Remembrance

and the

Design of Place

NUMBER SIX:
Sara and John Lindsey
Series in the Arts and Humanities

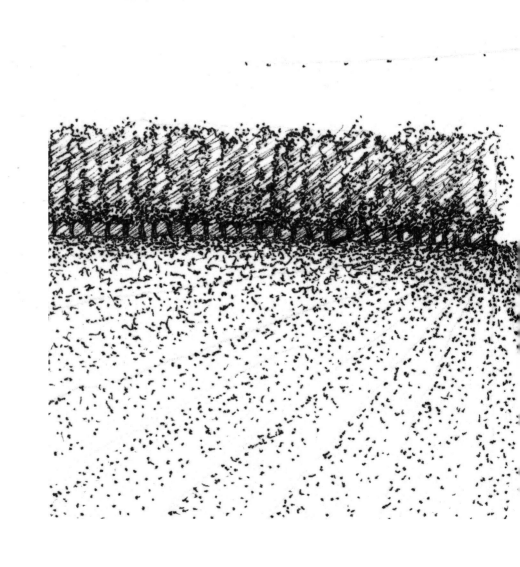

Remembrance
and the Design of Place

Frances Downing

TEXAS A&M UNIVERSITY PRESS
College Station

To all those who shared their memorable places;
illustrated and translated their thoughts about
the entanglement of memory and design;
and to those who often find themselves nesting in reverie,
divulging its meaning as the gift of architecture.

The paper used in this book
meets the minimum requirements
of the American National Standard
for Permanence of Paper for Printed
Library Materials, z39.48-1984.
Binding materials have been
chosen for durability.

*For a complete list of books in print in this series,
see the back of the book.*

Library of Congress Cataloging-in-Publication Data

Downing, Frances.
    Remembrance and the design of place / Frances Downing.
        p.   cm. — (Sara and John Lindsey series in the arts and
humanities ; no. 6)
        ISBN 0-89096-922-1 (cloth) — ISBN 0-89096-938-8 (pbk.)
        1. Architectural design—Psychological aspects.
    2. Architectural design—Methodology.   3. Memory.
    4. Place (Philosophy)   5. Architects—United States—
Interviews.   I. Title.   II. Series.
    NA2750.D68   2000
    720'.1—dc21   99-043690

Contents

Illustrations

Remembrance

and the

Design of Place

Chapter 1

The Content of Memory

WE ALL RETAIN MEMORIES OF PLACES. They identify who we are as individuals. At the same time, they tie us to networks of people, culture, and society. Even through time, they reach into the past to people whose lives and experiences were as real as ours, and into the future to those who lives we can only imagine.

I have always been fascinated by how talented architects are able to transfer the experiences of their own memorable places to future places without resorting to nostalgia or megalomania. How do they avoid these pitfalls? It seemed to me that the content of what designers transferred, the expression of these created places, must capture something significant, something that somehow touches us all and refers to our own basic experiences and identities. What we recognize in good architecture is what defines us as passionate, sensuous, intelligent humans.

These architects are not trying to resurrect the social or physical "past" from some nostalgic mist. Rather, they seek to interpret from their past experiences one of the defining elements of being human—namely, the lives we lead in places. The best designers seek to recreate transcendent experiences, to imagine other people and places, to breathe new life into something ancient and deepen our awareness of place making. This book traces the relationship between our experiences of memorable places and the expressive act of recreating them through design.

Like most designers, I have indulged myself in travel and visited all kinds of places: contemporary and historical, common and exalted. I have explored landscapes of great variety. Like everyone else, I retain in my memory significant places: places which surround me with a sense of well-being or make me recoil in distress or fear; places of vulnerability or power, of dependence or independence; places that satisfy my intellectual aspirations or present me with enigmas; places alive with sensuality; places that reflect my individuality or reveal my need for others. These memories of the places and events of my life provide a dynamic form of in-sight, and they present to my consciousness the experiential, emotional, and intellectual content of life as I know and feel it directly.

Susanne Langer's writing in two of her books, *Philosophy in a New Key* and *Feeling and Form,* has profoundly shaped certain of my key beliefs. The first is the idea that memorable mental images of place are symbolic of the lives we live, so woven in place. A second conviction is that these symbols are utilitarian—parts of our rational thinking processes—tying past experience to the present and to a potential future. In turn, Gerald Edelman's work in *Bright Air, Brilliant Fire,* has grounded my metaphoric feet, preventing me from roaming about, oblivious to our physical, biological realities. Edelman has been called a neural Darwinist—he puts the physical and the metaphysical worlds back together, fine-tuning the linkages between brain and mind. Both sources have proven essential as I framed the results of my research on memorable place experiences and their impact on the act of design.[1]

While the memorable places of my life have been invaluable to my designing mind, none define my *self* more profoundly than the California ranches, activities, and landscapes of my youth. California yielded many powerful landscape images. The trees that formed windbreaks in the San Joaquin Valley were not planted for their beauty. They were serviceable because their evergreen foliage was thick and unfriendly. They did, however, serve as homes for spiders, birds, small critters of all kinds, and my brothers. One brother in particular was hardy enough to invade these lines of soldier trees. Because they were not really suitable for tree houses, my brother and his friends dug elaborate tunnels between the trees and built forts and hideouts by placing boards over the tops of portions of their dugouts. They were meant to be secret. I was not invited. But I thought that everyone must have rows of trees. Growing up, I had no idea of their real purpose; eventually, however, their use became clear, as I experienced windy seasons in large square fields on open land. I have come to admit that I am unabashedly western in both substance and outlook. Yet I am capable of empathizing with people and places of diverse characters.

When I was a fledgling designer, I found it difficult to express or explain why these images of place were meaningful in my design life. They command my attention, sometimes because I call them from wherever they live and sometimes because they appear without conscious effort when I need their content, meaning, or presence to understand the content or context of a design task. My design life is populated by memories of experiences that

4

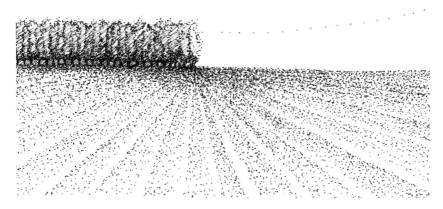

fig. 1. San Joaquin
Valley, by Frances
Downing

are, in most ways, peculiar to my own life. In deeper ways, however, these experiences present to me the essence of moments, events, places, or people that define my participation in the joys, disappointments, and conundrums of the human species.

My grandmother's kitchen is a place I identify with family retreats. It was a place where, in part, I became who I am and realized myself as part of the family fabric. It also was a place of sensuous delights, a place of fragrances: mouth-watering roasts, mashed potatoes, home-made breads, and pies to die for. The aroma of food was woven through the intimate dramas of our gatherings, making this "place" one my nose and mouth can recreate before my mind's eye can conjure it visually.

The kitchen was also a place of family history. By being small and quiet, I gained admission to confidences concerning other people's lives. If I stayed under the table long enough, eventually I would hear of heartbreak, love, hate, kindness, envy, adventure, and murder. The stories recounted in my grandmother's kitchen stretched to the horizons of my imagination. I could not confirm their veracity. These snatches of history, these confidences traded *sotto voce* and my furtive knowledge of them, however, framed my childhood with people, places, and events I felt I myself had experienced, if only vicariously.

Grandmother's kitchen, like all kitchens before and after, was a place

*Content
of Memory*

fig. 2.
Grandmother's
Kitchen, by Frances
Downing and Tom
Hubka

which collected people in all seasons, at all times of the day. I remember its dimensions and layout. I remember where the raisins were kept. I know that the window faced the east pastures and that, from it, you could see the hog barn and work yard. The light was intense in the mornings, soft in the evenings, and, over the course of the day, all degrees in between. I know the relationship of the kitchen wing to the rest of the house. I know this place. It is significant to me emotionally, experientially, and objectively. This is one of the conditions of memorable places: they are memorable for complex, densely interwoven reasons.

   We can transcend our own experiences by using them to imagine other people and places, to discover something new and surprising, and to deepen a thought. This ability demonstrates the power and potential that remembrance holds for us as we create future places. If we are to design, and teach others to design, places that are memorable and support a meaningful existence, we must first understand the essence and content that make a place memorable and how to transfer this content as we design. When we, as designers, understand how memorable experiences translate into meaningful inquiry and design strategies, this understanding points us toward fruitful conjectures and comparisons and helps us develop a broad range of conceivable avenues to pursue and evaluate. We complete a meaningful design cycle not only by prying our remembered past loose from its content, but also by imagining the future through referring to that past.

REMEMBRANCE AND MEMORY

There is a body of work that addresses memory as an arena of study, and some of this work informs us about the nature of remembrance. William Brewer, a noted author and imagery researcher, has qualified the different terms for memory, dividing them into personal memory, autobiographical facts, and recollective memory. *Personal memory* refers to the experiential aspect of memory; this is what I am addressing in this book. *Autobiographical facts* are those memories of places, people, and events from which all experiential quality is absent. Finally, *recollective memory* designates particular episodes in an individual's life.[2] All these definitions are relevant to the issues I discuss below. I was curious about the nature of specific places and events that remain with us for our entire lives and seem to impact the decisions that we as designers make during design inquiry.

The actual dating of these memories interested me in only the most general sense of "episodes" or "stages" in our lives. In particular, I wanted to know whether student designers were operating differently from professionals. Therefore, as I conducted my research, I noted whether images occurred before or after the individual entered architectural education. We commonly use temporal markers[3] (what house we lived in, with whom we lived, where we were, and so on) to designate significant life stages. The specific dating of recollective memories, however, does not seem to be meaningful in memory research beyond marking particular stages and episodes. Only "landmark events" have specific dates attached; otherwise, specific dating is of less meaning to recollection.

Researchers use autobiographical memory to indicate a larger set of memories that relate to self in its many dimensions.[4] Recollective memory, then, forms a subset of autobiographical memory. Through his own work

Content of Memory

and that of others, researcher and author Martin Conway[5] establishes that both autobiographical and recollective memories are processed constructively; that is, the act of remembering reflects a complex cycling and sampling of an extensive knowledge base. The act of recollection is never "complete" in the sense that all information is present. Rather, information is filtered at the time of the original event and refiltered at the time of recollection. A sense of "pastness" is achieved through either a feeling of knowing or the experience of remembering.[6]

These two ways—knowing and remembering, recollective memory and autobiographical memory—are mirrored by the construction of remembrances as either "field" memories or "observer" memories. Field memories are those that retain an original point of view and very little emotion. Observer memories, on the other hand, are noted as events which encode higher emotions and in which a person can "see" himself or herself within the image. "Field memories [are] recollective memory images that represented the original scene from the viewpoint from which it was originally experienced . . . Observer memories [are] recollective memory images that represented the original scene as an external observer might have seen it." Brewer defines recollective memory as encompassing more than a simple visual image. Rather, it encapsulates an individual's "whole state of mind" at the moment of the original episode or event, as it was experienced.[7]

There is a difference between simply "naming" a memorable place and searching memory for its meaning. I asked designers to work in two stages, naming places from memory, then sorting them to elicit meaning. The difference between field memories and observer memories may relate to the different states of mind that designers in my research exhibited. It may be that, when designers simply identify a past place experience, they remember through a specific point of view. If they then are asked to contemplate the *meaning* of a particular place memory, rather than simply to communicate it, they need to reconstruct the image in an "observer" mode by virtually moving about the space and seeing it with intention.

NAMING, CONTEMPLATING, AND REASONING

Distinctions among naming, contemplating, and reasoning became meaningful when I noticed varying "ways" in which designers responded to the tasks I set for them. I began my investigation of the relationship between memory and design by interviewing more than 150 architects and student designers. I started by asking them simple questions to launch them on a journey through their own past place experiences. Next, I had them name the images of memorable places they reconstructed in their minds. I recorded the names of these memories on three-by-five index cards. In the second stage, I asked the designer to look at the cards for her or his places and categorize each one according to a broad theme that expressed some quality that was essential to the individual and the remembered place. The designer then continued to categorize and recategorize the whole bank of cards until he or she ran out of themes that seemed meaningful.[8]

I began to realize that the design of my research would force an analytic tracing of general relationships among the interviewees' memorable places. Although this was, in fact, my aim and the things that I discovered were extremely useful, I couldn't "record" the holistic content of memorable experience as it *presented* itself to the consciousness of each participant. Slowly it dawned on me that somehow I was missing the power of the act of remembrance as I pursued more analytical concerns about memory. I realized, too, that capturing this elusive quality and translating it into words that conveyed the content of in-sight would be a complex undertaking indeed. It is only indirectly, then, that I can refer to the acts of remembrance I witnessed.

During these interviews, I noticed a phenomenon to which neither I nor the interviewee ever referred. While the act of remembering was something I could observe to a certain extent, I could make no scientific assertions about what was happening. Even now I can report only what *appeared* to be happening. There seemed to be three different acts of "expression." One had to do with *naming* remembered places. Another expressive form was related to the mental image of place in the participants' minds as they *contemplated* its meaning. A third act of expression was the *"reasoning"* of meaningful categories.

I began each interview by informing the architect or student designer that the activities in which we would be engaged would have two stages— naming and sorting—and that he or she should not tell me *how* each memorable place was meaningful until we reached the sorting phase. After the designers finished "naming" the places, I asked them to perform a sorting task that would help me understand what kinds of things they considered meaningful about these places. Of course, it was never this simple. Often, simply naming a place caused participants to muse about its meaning; in fact, this was the rule rather than the exception.

In any case, there was a striking difference in their demeanors when they "named" a place, when they assigned meaning to the categories they formed, and when they contemplated the significance of a particular place. When naming a place, the designers would sit still, focus inward, search for the memorable place, and assign a name to it—grandfather's garage, Fallingwater, the field behind my house, a room in a Paris boardinghouse, a scene from *Blade Runner,* and so on. Forming categories, on the other hand, was an intellectual exercise involving reasoning and communication, even when the domain being formed included emotional or experiential content.

When the designers were asked to "label" the categories or domains they formed, however, interesting discussions ensued. This task was difficult for several of the designers. They often formed domains through a kind of emotional response to which it was difficult to assign words or terms that reflected the order they had created in front of them. Finally, however, the participants adopted a reasoning attitude, expressing what they believed to be meaningful through the use of language that they thought would provide clarification. They did not hesitate to name objective characteristics that represented "concepts" of form and order that they had learned in school and honed during practice. Experiential constructions of place were more complex, yet fairly easily intellectualized and named. However, designers found it most difficult to name or label emotionally charged constructs clearly.

When the designers sought to understand the significance of a particular place image by discussing it in detail, they displayed a different behavior. Their eyes moved around the space we occupied, as if reconstructing or "seeing" the imagined place. They were "in" the places as they described their meaning—whether in viewpoint they were stationary or actually moving about in the imagined place is still a mystery. What I hadn't foreseen was that the act of remembrance would be a powerful holistic experience. I realized that *remembrance is not particularly an act of knowledge, but rather is an act of in-sight*—of "seeing" or conceptualizing meaning within experience. Memory suspends our past experiences and allows us to draw them rationally to the forefront of our imaginations. The designers presented memorable experiences directly to consciousness, where they were free to grasp, realize, comprehend, or ignore the meaning that the experiences contained.

AMBIVALENCE OF CONTENT

Recategorizing images to fit different thematic "sorts" implies that the meaning of memorable places is never fixed; rather, as these experiences are mixed with active conception, they may be manipulated to satisfy all kinds of present needs. Memorable imagery has an ambivalence of content rarely found in words and narrative. It is not knowledge or communication that is conveyed during this act; instead, it is a rediscovery of internalized meaning. It is not the theme, accuracy, or fantasies of a memory that stirred these designers, but the capacity of a memorable experience to present human feeling, to present life in its very being: its power, routine, surprise, and sadness. Whatever the effect—amazement and delight or isolation and fear—the thing that is "understood" or expressed by the mental imagery of memorable places is not discursive; it is direct, entire, and presentational.

Both from my observations and from the categorizations of place formed by the designers, it was clear that memorable experiences are stored symbolically, not materially as empirical snapshots.[9] Designers often reconstructed memorable experiences of place, sometimes in full scale within the space we occupied, through some mental capacity to structure its presence. However, there was never any indication that the designers were completing an image; rather, they tended to remember specific contents and their interpreted meanings. While the mental image is holistic in nature, this does not translate to "correctness" or even any particular reference to a "truthful" reconstruction. Memories do not represent a record of *exact* pictures in the mind—they are, instead, symbolic, because they present to us through mental imagery the life we have lived in physical space.

SYMBOLIC MEANING: AN EXPRESSION OF LIFE

A mental image is a virtual object; its sensate character is its entire being. Likewise, a memorable experience stands apart from everyday experience, and its appearance constitutes its pure quality. What emerges from memorable experience is the symbol of sentience, of life in all its conflicts and meanings.[10] The places designers remember capture the significance of experience as contact, retreat, love, joy, fear, inadequacy, empathy, grace, intelligence, order; as membership in a social fabric; and as vessel for cultural meaning. For my investigation, what is significant about a memorable place experience is not the actual feeling, but the *ideas* of feeling which *present* meaning to designers, who may find in the experience the stimulus for creating new places.

In California, I grew up around weekend visits to water reservoirs. These places were like rewards for my father, who all week long was shut up inside a hot mechanic's shop. The reservoirs were numerous, and I had no idea how the landscape had been transformed between the time my great-aunts had moved to Los Angeles and just after World War II, when I was born into a wantonly created landscape.

To me these structures always had existed, and the landscape always had been dotted by great hydroelectric monsters. As a family, we took advantage of these places on Sundays—they were our religion of sun and water. This landscape marks my early ideas about the capability of humans to trans-

fig. 3. California Reservoirs, by Frances Downing

form—to "make," sometimes in a crude way, as in the raggedy canals where I learned to swim, and sometimes in an elegant way, as in the great engineered waterways spilling from dams. After all, the water we used was there for politically weighted irrigation of the orange groves, grape vineyards, and cotton fields of my youth. Everything all around me was created, groomed, and cultivated—and water was the key to it all. Water symbolized the power to manipulate a whole ecosystem.

Symbolic memory is uniquely human. Other animals may be able to conceptualize, but their ability to remember symbols and their associated meanings is limited. The evolution of symbols in higher-order consciousness[11] serves the primary consciousness (that which is tied to the immediate and overwhelming present). Symbolization requires an ability to construct a socially based selfhood in order that the world be modeled in terms of "others," of the past and the future. A state of *direct awareness* of the relationships among past, present, and future can be achieved only through higher-order consciousness. Without symbolic memory, this capacity is impossible and cannot develop. The gift of symbolic memory enables us to be humans who elaborate, refine, connect, create, and remember.[12]

The physical mapping of unique experience creates individuals who never can be replicated. While the workings of our minds may seem an evident mystery, one thing is clear: memory and all its consequences are central to our identity, to our ability to reason and value, and to both our semantic and our image-based thought processes. When I first sat down with professional architects and student designers to elicit their sets of memorable places and to try to make sense of the content of memorable place imagery and its role in design, I was faced with powerful imagery that spoke of each person's independent existence. The place experiences they considered memorable—Hagia Sophia, a bedroom in Kansas, Rossi's cemetery, a highway in Peru, the pueblos near Santa Fe, an uncle's tractor barn, a tree house—were idiosyncratic, varying greatly among individuals. Each set, each bank of images, was the embodiment of a person's experiences. From such experiences—both direct experiences and influences from surroundings—are built a set of values. In turn, as personal, societal, and cultural values form, an individual begins to shape experiences in return. An individual begins to "see" and "understand" the world through complex filters. Behaviors and memories follow physical paths in each brain, reinforcing some and weakening others, making each individual unique yet connected to others.

Memory, in its broadest definition, is tied holistically to our bodies as they exist in and are of this world. In our lifetimes, we develop a selective system of molecules, cells, and specialized organs that have memory and define our biological, emerging, and changing selves, each of us distinct from everyone else, none ever repeated or replicated in any exact form.[13] The immune system depends on the memory of "self" in order to reject whatever is non-self. Aldo Rossi makes this point in *A Scientific Autobiography:* "Specificity cannot exist without memory, nor can memory [exist] that does not emanate from a specific moment: only the union of the two permits the awareness of one's own individuality and its opposite (of *self* and *non-self*)."[14] So we stand, reach, touch, see, hear, smell, shout, and whisper our own existence, gathering our particular experiences within our growing sense of self. The non-self world is not just a necessary "other"; it *is* our experience, our existence, our life. This world is *embodied* by us.

Content of Memory

Our self/non-self evolves and changes through an interaction that involves reflex learning and true learning, both of which entail perceptual categorization and recategorization of phenomena. Reflex categorizations take place in primary consciousness, while true-learning categorizations of phenomena and symbolic referencing take place in higher-order consciousness.[15]

Memory is an essential property of all these biological self/non-self relationships. Each individual memory evolves and helps select perceptual phenomena to add to the arsenal of knowledge and meaning built over time through idiosyncratic experience and human will. A person is not simply a *tabula rasa,* as past conceptualizations of our relationship to the world suggested. As non-self impinges upon self, the self makes decisions, values some experience over others, reconstructs experience, and produces a "will" that acts upon the non-self world in a creative and ongoing interaction.

Place images are integral to each individual, and the power they possess as specific images defines an individual's identity. It would be impossible for me to convey another person's act of remembrance or the power of a particular place without diluting its significance with my own interpretation. Various artists, however, have produced excellent accounts of the remembrance of memorable places and experiences.

Marcel Proust explored the *Remembrance of Things Past* in the introduction to *Swann's Way.*[16] His descriptions of place are rich and compelling. I use them here to explore relationships among memory, image, and identity. In the last part of the chapter "Overture," the adult Proust describes sitting down to tea and *petite madeleines* with his family:

> And soon, mechanically, weary after a dull day with the prospect of a depressing morrow, I raised to my lips a spoonful of the tea in which I had soaked a morsel of the cake. No sooner had the warm liquid, and the crumbs with it, touched my palate than a shudder ran through my whole body, and I stopped, intent upon the extraordinary changes that were taking place. An exquisite pleasure had invaded my senses, but individual, detached, with no suggestion of its origin. And at once the vicissitudes of life had become indifferent to me, its disasters innocuous, its brevity illusory—this new sensation having had on me the effect which love has of filling me with a precious essence; or rather this essence was not in me, it was myself.[17]

In this instance, it is the sensation of taste, likely mixed with aroma, that triggers Proust's journey into his past experiences. It is not unusual for a modal shift beginning with one sensation to open the door, so to speak, to complex mental images of places, occasions, and people. Mental images can be formed from any sensate beginning. For me, the smell of mothballs always shifts my consciousness back to my Great-aunt LuLu's guest room, with its clean, aromatic sheets. This smell of mothballs begins a cascade of complex memories of my parents, my great-aunt's house and possessions, and the occasions we spent together. In their concentration on visual and kinesthetic experience, architects often forget just how strong mental images of aroma, taste, and sound can be. Without some of these considerations—unless other sensory dimensions are taken into consideration—the places that are made may remain "flat."

For Proust, the elusive memory is not the "virtual" object which Langer describes as separable from self and intelligible apart from self.[18] Rather, it *is* self. It seems to me, however, that memory is both non-self and self. Obviously, a memory of place cannot be separated from our bodies unless we choose to express it physically—in a drawing, poem, sculpture, architecture, music, literature, and so on. This expressed object, however, is outside the body and now takes on its own evolving significance, apart from the original memory. If the expressed object captures the "life" of experience, it has captured significant *form.* The original mental image, according to Langer, is "virtual"—not a thing—but she indicates that it, as a virtual object, can be set aside and contemplated. I believe we are capable of contemplating the virtual object but am less sure that it can be cleanly set aside. My understanding of the mental images generated by architects is that they are endlessly complex and connected to self/non-self in multiple ways. We might be able to tease out important in-sights and understandings at one time, while at another time the memorable place experience might suggest a completely different meaning. Time moves on, circumstances change, and our own memories evolve. For Proust, memories captured by taste dance at the edge of consciousness, teasing and haunting him:

> Undoubtedly what is thus palpitating in the depths of my being must be the image, the visual memory which, being linked to that taste, has tried to follow it into my conscious mind. But its struggles are too far off, too much confused; scarcely can I perceive the colourless reflection in which are blended the uncapturable whirling medley of radiant hues, and I cannot distinguish its form, cannot invite it, as the one possible interpreter, to translate to me the evidence of its contemporary, its inseparable paramour, the taste of cake soaked in tea; cannot ask it to inform me what special circumstance is in question, of what period in my past life.[19]

This struggle is clearly one with which we can all identify: a slippery, out-of-focus fragment at the edge of consciousness, escaping our calculating attempts to capture it, teasing us with its familiarity, exasperating us with its elusiveness. The mind grants us bits and pieces of memorable imagery at certain times, while at others memories explode into consciousness in full color, self-propelled, and without justification. We cannot always "reason" their existence or "conceive" their meaning. In this process, cause is not always followed by effect, nor is effect conceptually bound to cause. The retrieval cycles described in the general literature reflect this process of cycling through our memory of a place or occasion until an image is constructed to the degree necessary for that moment. For Proust, "suddenly the memory returns. The taste was that of the little crumb of madeleine which on Sunday mornings at Combray (because on those mornings I did not go out before church time), when I went to say good day to her in her bedroom, my Aunt Leone used to give me, dipping first in her own cup of real or of lime-flower tea. The sight of the little madeleine had recalled nothing to my mind before I tasted it; perhaps because I had so often seen such things in the interval."[20]

Proust realizes that a sensation in the present moment, a taste, can immediately connect us, through our own capacities for imaginative reconstruction, to a past that waits to offer us its meaning. The notion that memories "pop" into existence is one described by researchers who see memories as background material that emerges into conscious awareness in response to a stimulus in a present condition.[21]

Imagination and the act of remembrance are tied together irrevocably, as each of us gathers the bits and pieces of memory and builds them into a more holistic recollection. It is not important that the memory be eidetically correct. Akhter Ahsen[22] suggests that the mental image not only contains perceptual memories, such as visual impressions, fragrances, tastes, kinesthetic sensations, and sounds, but also presents parables for meaning. The mental image is a self-portrait of secret wishes and desires, as well as the ground for common cultural (and, some claim, species-wide) values and assumptions. In the design world, one of the most critical attributes of memory and the mental image is the designer's ability to interact dramatically with the mental image, adjusting its meaning and drawing from it complex relationships— emotive, experiential, and objective. The mental image, therefore, presents a personal biography as well as a vehicle enabling the designer to manipulate future projects.

Stimulated by taste, Proust created images that presented the reconstructed actions and feelings of the individuals involved, and the setting for those experiences: "But when from a long-distant past nothing subsists, after the people are dead, after the things are broken and scattered, still, alone, more fragile, but with more vitality, more insubstantial, more persistent, more faithful, the smell and taste of things remain poised a long time, like souls, ready to remind us, waiting and hoping for their moment, amid the ruins of all the rest; and bear unfaltering, in the tiny and almost impalpable drop of their essence, the fast structure of recollection."[23] Within Proust's memory of that occasion exists a confirmation of the relationship between memory and imagination, and between mental image and identity. The remembered past acts as one of the primary conduits for imagination and the expression of emotion, experience, and intellect within a bounded phenomenon.[24]

Langer suggests that images "fill" the virtual space between us and real objects. Mental images are created through our imaginations and differ from immediate physical acts that we also produce and simply live. Mental images are different because they satisfy a symbolic function: they mediate between the self and the non-self.[25] It is this capacity that holds incredible value for the designer. The remembered images of place not only define the individual but also place the individual within a context, with values, and in relationships with "others."

Proust believed that the past was captured within sensations that material objects might provoke at any time, and he believed that the *essence* of past experience is transferred to the present through memory:

And once I had recognized the taste of the crumb of madeleine soaked in her decoction of lime-flowers which my aunt used to give me (although I did not yet know and must long postpone the discovery of why the memory made me so happy), immediately the old grey house upon the street, where her room was, rose up like the scenery of a theater to attach itself to the little pavilion, opening on to the garden, which had been built out behind it for my parents (the isolated panel which until that moment had been all that I could see); and with the house the town, from morning to night and in all weathers, the Square where I was sent before luncheon, the streets along which I used to run errands, the country roads we took when it was fine. And just as the Japanese amuse themselves by filling a porcelain bowl with water and steeping in it little crumbs of paper which until then are without character or form, but, the moment they become wet, stretch themselves and bend, take on colour and distinctive shape, become flowers or houses or people, permanent and recognizable, so in the moment all the flowers in our garden and M. Swann's park, and the water-lilies on the Vivonne and the good folk of the village and their little dwellings and the parish church and the whole of Combray and of its surroundings, taking their proper shapes and growing solid, sprang into being, town and gardens alike, from my cup of tea.[26]

Content of Memory

17

We all carry with us a bank of memorable places; like Proust's experience, they visit us, remind us, comprise us, and connect us. The *Remembrance of Things Past,* for Proust, never was about sentimentality; rather, the emergent images were a kind of art stimulated by sensuous encounters with mundane, daily occurrences. An imaginative deliberation that escaped the languor of "habit" was a triumph for seeking the essence of living. Each of us, developing within the powerful constrictions of history, language, and culture that form our world views and help create our value systems, still is capable, through memory and a powerful ability imaginatively to recollect past experience, of developing as an individual with a discrete identity. Each individual is at once a product of both social and biological development, yet is mortal and unpredictably creative.[27]

Consciousness is being conscious of self. It simply *is.* This capacity depends upon our representation of self, upon our need to create a social self, upon our action in the environment, and upon an evolving model of the past and its relationship to the present and to the potential future. Consciousness is the very richness of social communication that allows us to form our values and understand ourselves in, and as a part of, the environment. Architects tend to frame this knowledge of self through places that are value-laden yet fluid in their meanings. As we respond to and reflect others, we generate self-consciousness as a necessary result. Value systems, which underlie the aims and purposes of each individual, rise from the development of a social self. Yet, according to Edelman,[28] we can escape biology to a certain degree in order to modify our values. The element of *will* is sufficiently present in human interactions for the future to remain open rather than predetermined; by remembering what was, we are able to imagine what can be.

DOMAINS OF PLACE EXPERIENCE

In the process of recording over 150 interviews, it became obvious to me that certain themes were present in each individual's set of experiences. These themes I call *domains,* and I explore them in chapter 2. Although each of the many place images the designers produced was unique, certain domains appeared again and again: the secret place, the Arcadian place, the ancestral place, the shared place, the alone place, the intimate place, the gregarious place, places that stretch to meet the horizon line, and places that enclose and protect. These domains arose from designers' own mental constructions. These constructions, however, were fluid. Designers placed the same image in more than one domain, suggesting that the memories they have of places are complex enough to have multiple meanings. Designers feel free to categorize and recategorize memorable place experiences in relation to present ideas and potential futures.

In the next chapter, I also introduce some of the results from a game which a colleague, Joe Self, and I designed and presented in various places during the past five years.[29] We called the game "Spatial Solitaire." Its purpose was to elicit from the participants a scenario that would allow each person to use a memorable image of a past place in a limited design situation. We asked participants to create a character (the character could be a real person, a historical figure, an imagined person, and so on) and an act in which the character was engaged. They were to remember a place from their own past that would assist them in some way in designing a place for this act that the character performed. These drawings represent a twenty- to thirty-minute commitment to this process, so they are original sketch problems.

Later I asked the participants to write a very short essay offering their opinion and expertise concerning the relationship of memorable places and design. Some essays are about the specific design and are personal statements about the particular memories and their meaning. Other essays are more theoretical. The essays are included as appendices to this book, and I will refer to them as the book unfolds.

SIGNIFICANT FORM OF MEMORABLE PLACE EXPERIENCES

The third chapter of this book discusses the significant form of experiences. What domains capture for momentary contemplation is the significant form that is symbolic of communal experiences, each experience being idiosyncratic in its own right yet "belonging" to a functional domain. Here the term *functional* does not mean "conveniently arranged." Rather, it denotes a realm of sentient activities, "a system of interlocking and intersecting actions, a continuous functional pattern."[30] Architects create significant form from memorable places only if they discover and understand the patterns held within their seemingly unique memories—that is, the functional realms of contact, retreat, love, joy, fear, inadequacy, empathy, grace, intelligence, and order, to name a few. In the practice of architecture, the ability to transcend one's own experience without losing sight of the potential for reference to the design task in the immediate present always has constituted part of each designer's struggle. Those who succeed rediscover powerful places, use that understanding in present conditions, and create new places that are fresh and memorable containers of significant life experiences.

Content of Memory

CONTENT OF EXPERIENTIAL METAPHORIC REFERENCE

In the designer's expressions of the content of memorable places, the use of *metaphoric reference* is related to experience. We experience our world through our bodies—i.e., in an "embodied" state. Not surprisingly, when we attempt to explain and explore the content of places, our memories of them, and the potential for understanding them communally, we use metaphors drawn from the physical world in which the body orients, values, substantiates, contains, and personifies our experiences. Metaphoric references pervade our lives, language, and expressions of meaning.[31]

In chapter 4, I explore the content of experiential metaphoric reference. Designers *conceive* of places predominantly through metaphors. This is clear from the verbal expressions they made during this research. Their language is permeated with metaphor and presents evidence of prevalent patterns in the way they think about places.

INTENTIONAL FRAMEWORKS FOR TRANSFER OF MEANING

Intentional frameworks for meaning, treated in chapter 5, suggest ways designers orient their memories of places experientially, emotionally, and intellectually. These three frameworks for meaning are fluid, much like the domains mentioned earlier. Designers are capable of "framing" their memory of a place through one or all three ways of orienting place memories. This ability to make references to memories consciously or unconsciously through frameworks also is structured through individual will and intention. Designers construct and reconstruct references to get at the meaning of experience as it relates to the task at hand. Designers thus can direct their attention and move in a fluid manner from one framework to another, reconstructing images through experiential, emotional, or intellectual filters.

IMAGINATION AND INNOVATION

This book ultimately is about the use of memorable images in the act of design. I therefore must refer to case studies and theories of imagination and innovation that are drawn from the practice of design. If theory is not grounded in action, irresponsible speculation becomes a danger. Therefore I cite examples of professionals at work in design and their obvious reliance upon precedents (analogies) and prototypes (metaphors) to structure the design act. I include the "conceptual" drawings from a project completed by Kallman, McKinnell, and Wood for the American Academy of Arts and

Sciences. This project was published in the November, 1981, issue of *Architectural Record.*[32] I use it here because the drawings are illustrative of the domains introduced in chapter 2, as well as the process of design covered in chapters 4 and 5. Through the use of these examples, memory emerges as an inexact process based on association and generalization. While memory is never replicative, it is dynamic.[33] A theory of imagination and innovation is introduced in chapter 6.

CONNECTIONS AMONG PAST, PRESENT, AND FUTURE

Architects act as bridges linking the past with the present and the future. They establish a continuity of human interaction with place, as time unfolds and the tenor of change seems overwhelming. Through the act of designing, the architect provides a passage between past places and future places that can be mapped carefully and debated openly. Our ability to clear this passage or path is a necessary condition for forming meaningful acts in design. A greater understanding on the part of designers of their own crafts and patterns should ensure a rich, diverse environment for all of us. The connections among past, present, and future are examined in chapter 7.

*Content
of Memory*

Chapter 2

Domains of Place Experience

ESPITE THE COMPLEX individuality that originates in idiosyncratic life experiences, significant and recurring domains emerge when designers are asked to create meaningful order from their bank of memorable places. It was only after I had detected the domains present in the image banks of designers that I was reminded of Langer's definition of functional realms. Domains are the *form* to which a particular functional realm belongs. A *functional realm* is a "system of interlocking and intersecting actions"—a pattern of sentient behavior in place. Domains therefore symbolize qualities, actions, and stories of significance: contact, retreat, participation, identity, love, grace, sensuousness, intellect, intimacy, growth, expansiveness, reflection, communing, and more. A domain, then, is not functional in a traditional sense of architectural programming, in which a space is designed to meet its stated function (office, kitchen, bathroom, etc.). Rather, places are defined by the life one lives and its significance to place. Place becomes the framework of living which rests between logic and biography and in which "function" remains the framework of "life." Ahsen defines memorable mental images as presenting parables of meaning in which moral or spiritual relations are set forth.[1]

An example of moral values held in place experience as mental imagery is supplied by a participant in the game of Spatial Solitaire. John Williams (appendix 1) tells a tale of the parrot who rudely reminds the people in a community that they must avoid being "hypocrites." The screeching of this word from a neighbor's porch on Sunday mornings is an exotic reminder to citizens to be constantly on guard against such a condition. Williams then produces a college campus which benefits from rude parrots screeching "Hypocrite" at unexpected moments, reminding hearers that even institutions must avoid this pitfall.

Within the sketch the following handwritten labels appear: Parrot, Stadium, Parking, Library, adm, Parrot, Arch, any, campus, Parrot, Old main, John Wms U. of Ark.

fig. 4. Parrot System, by John Williams

When I was growing up in Van Buren, Arkansas, one of our neighbors owned a parrot. On warm days she would move the parrot to the front porch, where he could observe the street and the passersby. On Sunday mornings, as we were going to church, the parrot would scream the word "hypocrite" at us. At first it seemed humorous, but soon I noticed that it seemed to make some of us uncomfortable. I asked my dad what the word meant. He explained that a hypocrite was someone who did not practice what he preached or thought. It had to do with integrity—in a person or even an institution. It seemed to me that any institution, including a university, should be reminded constantly to check its own integrity. Therefore, [I include] stations for parrots to scream out now and then the word "hypocrite" so that the institution might check itself (appendix 1).

Phenomenologists believe that, as we describe the use we make of any particular object (for our purposes, the "objects" to be addressed are memorable images of place), we also *intuit its essence*—that is, *the underlying form* that makes a place "what it is."[2] "Fundamentally, we do not *know about* objects in the world; we *use* them, and the problem for the phenomenologist is to explain how it is that we can withdraw ourselves from our tools in order to look at them as things."[3] The domains cited here are significant form "realized" through particular places—each a reference to a functional realm. Designers in this study grouped and defined significant form through the domains they created from seemingly diverse experiences. We come to "know about" the world through these changing and evolving domains.

It is important to note that domains do not represent a classical typology. Although we all use "types" as a way of categorizing and recategorizing our experiences, the domains presented here are loosely organized functional realms. The creation of typologies suggests that there are sets of classical characteristics that can be identified as being essential to the type. Edelman, however, suggests that typologies should not be understood in a classical sense. Rather, our consciousness arises from an evolutionary process, rather than through recognition of tight typological categories.[4]

Recollective memory is defined by many researchers as "a particular episode in an individual's life."[5] The episodes I elicited from designers were place-oriented and specialized, compared to the broad implications in the field of memory research.[6] However, a compelling correspondence emerged between the memorable places I was pursuing and the results that evolved. Since designers were able to recollect and name "memorable" experiences in place, one can conclude that there is some significance tied to each episode of memory. Researchers have, in fact, found that emotion inundates the act of recollection—indeed, any performance based on memorability. It is highly emotional events that tend to "stand out" from ordinary memory. One could suppose, then, that all the place images mentioned by the designers in this study were charged with a fair amount of emotion.

Goal attainment is a prominent feature of lifetime periods and plays an important role in memorability.[7] Lifetime periods can be thought of as general structures for thematic events—for example, work, play, relationships to others, relationships to places, actions, activities, and so on. These thematic periods are general structures to which a person associates whatever he or she is remembering. Encoding an event in memory is thought to be tied to these themes in complex, interwoven structures. The "accuracy" of memorable places is by nature incomplete. Their viability as a record of previous selves, times, and places, however, has a certain level of assurance and accuracy. If this were not the case, we would be unable to tap past experience to order the present and future in any constructive sense. The "looseness" afforded by this uncertainty and bearable inaccuracy is valuable, because it allows the construction and reconstruction of memorable place experience through different compositions of meaning.[8]

When I asked designers to categorize their memorable past place experiences according to similarities and themes that were important to them, they constructed the system of domains presented here. Constructions of meaning relate to the designers' cognition of the world (a personal system of logic) and to their ability systematically to group meaningful experiences into varying domains that they valued.[9] Personal summaries are a necessary feature of memory, since we cannot remember eidetically—that is, we cannot produce a complete, literal, or objective record.

The domains which individual designers identified for memorable places turned out to be commonly held understandings shared across groups of individual designers at all the different stages of professional development represented in this study. The importance of different domains depended upon the maturity of the designer; however, all the domains were present and expressed by student designers and architects alike. While idiosyncratic systems of logic may be present, I concentrated on finding strains of meaning that indicated whether or not there were common constructions for memorable places. Here it became evident that the information I collected about memorable place imagery contained material that is central to the life of a designer. Indeed, the reasons for many of the designers' career choices were bound up with the names and histories of places written on the small white cards we produced.

THE DOMAINS
Secret Places

All designers cherish a domain that dates from their youth: the secret places or hiding places that served as retreats for themselves or for themselves and a select few. These generally begin as child-constructed places in the landscape

fig. 5. Iowa, by
Frances Downing

(tree houses and fortresses of various materials); "claimed" manmade constructions such as aqueducts, partially walled spaces, and created landscapes; or imaginative extensions of an *intimate forest* of "found" natural places such as meadows, the edges of a body of water, or the undersides of fantastic bushes or trees.

When I was very young, we lived in Iowa for a few years. My parents were from the Midwest, and Iowa allowed access to extended family on both sides. The landscape in southern Iowa was created by moraines left by the last Ice Age, creating a seemingly endless rolling landscape rich in hillocks and gullies and perfect for play. Here were trees that called out for jerry-rigged structures to be built, where mulberries could be eaten that would stain the skin and clothes of children who could not be reasoned with. Vines hung from trees, allowing us to pretend a Tarzan-like existence. In the fields, rows of corn created spaces narrow and high, unlike any space I could find inside the large cowbarns or Victorian farmhouses. I would venture into the seemingly ordered universe of the fields with some trepidation.

The image that Karen Cordes Spence generated in response to the Spatial Solitaire game is a secret place. The childhood backyards and near neighborhoods of most of the designers whom I interviewed contained a plethora of hiding places or group hiding places. Karen's memory of her own backyard incorporates the gross distortion of scale so common in a child's perception and/or imagination. She remembers large boulders, multiple trees, and protected views. On a revisit, she finds the objective scale quite different from what she remembers. Nevertheless, childhood memories of secret escapes are powerful. Her use of such a memory to inform design about the nature of retreat is not surprising. The act of retreat and the essence of secret places are bound inextricably together, whether we are children or adults. A memory such as this one is the only way we can carry an understanding of the human desire to retreat, to retrench, to find ourselves, and to daydream. It is necessary that a designer understand this basic human need, and the only means of doing so is buried within our experience of such need. It is the designer's own in-sight into meaningful experience that is carried by the mental image.

This place is for Dorothy in *The Wizard of Oz.* Dorothy is a strong character whom I remember from my childhood, an ordinary girl who had powers beyond her own recognition. The memorable elements that anchor this place for Dorothy are also from my childhood: the overgrown vines, the rocks, and the large oak trees provided an environment that I imagined as jungle trails, magnificent houses, boats, islands, treacherous roads, and infallible lookouts when I was young. My backyard had unlimited possibilities. The place for Dorothy begins from such unlimited possibilities (as all designs do), taking the shape of a simple wood structure that provides a space for many activities. It is a place to look, to sit, to imagine, to pretend, and to just be. It may be anything that one desires, like the elements in a childhood backyard. The wood structure

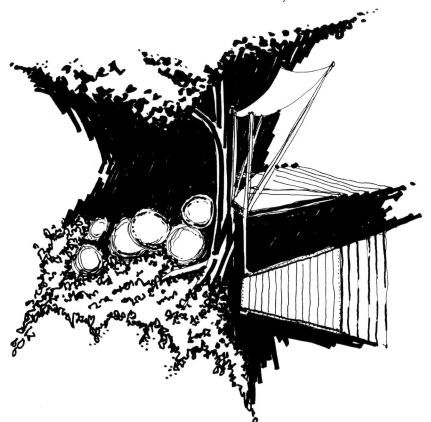

fig. 6. Dorothy, by Karen Cordes Spence

27

is raised above the land to provide Dorothy with a view of the world around, yet it also has stairs to enable her to go wherever she chooses. (Karen Cordes Spence, appendix 2)

Built forms of this domain often were places that were unfinished—attics, root cellars, or under the stairs. Often their unfinished nature provided a sense of ownership through an ability to complete the place with one's presence. Closets and large furniture also were important to this category.

A secret place always has aspects of a "removed" existence, being a place that, physically or mentally, is created for retreat, intimacy, enclosure, screening, and protection. These often are places of power and control that cannot be known or invaded by "outside" forces.

A tree house, one frequently mentioned secret place, is a good example of all the characteristics discussed above. Tree houses are removed from the ground plane. Often they are made by the occupant. The tree screens, encloses, and protects the existence of the secret place. There often is a control mechanism for entry, or entry is made to be complex or dangerous. Power emanates from taking up a position of which others are unaware or which they cannot attain.

As a domain, *secret places* include places named in adult experiences, but less frequently and perhaps with less "fantastic" associations. Adult designers tended to name *alone places* or sometimes *intimate places* and place them within the same categories as youthful *secret places.* Often mature designers would have "metaphoric" tree houses—places removed, remote, and defensible from "outsiders." *Secret places,* therefore, remain an important domain throughout the designers' lifetimes. It seems, however, that places of youthful retreat retain the most powerful associations within this domain.

Ancestral Places

Designers identify another domain that emerges from childhood. *Ancestral places* are retrieved from extended family interactions and can engage the landscape as much as built forms. Some ancestral places are Arcadian places: pastoral images of farms, ranches, and familial retreats. Townscapes are mentioned within the realm of extended families and seem to be favored for their sense of social connection and cultural meaning. Experiences that refer to special people also signify ancestral places: Grandmother's kitchen, an aunt's porch, a workroom filled with tools, an uncle's tractor barn, a father's chair, and numerous significant rooms and gardens. This domain contains multiple aspects of communion, intimate and/or gregarious, active or static, open

fig. 7. Tree House, by Frances Downing

or closed, comforting or discomfiting. The most significant attribute common to all ancestral places is the definition of personal identity within a realm shared with familiar others. The intimacy or aggravation of a familial "nest," made by others but surrounding and defining the individual, allows ancestral places to organize young lives and instill personal, social, and cultural values.

Wes Janz utilizes an ancestral place to frame a design for a workshop. The character in his game of Spatial Solitaire is John D. Rockefeller III, whose act is to hire an architect. Here the designer refers to his father's workshop on his family farm. The organization of this place is remembered and holds some sense of what it is to "work" with the "tools" at hand. This memory is simultaneously a fragment of his father's life space, identity, and familiarity, and a precedent for work. These two aspects of this place are intertwined and mean each other. Ancestral places often fix our own identities with the people and places of our developing years. The idea that "work" can be identified this way has a message for young people. It seems to make no difference that Wes is an architect and not a farmer like his father. The idea of an organized existence where any tool can be found to answer a current need is one definition of what it is to do "work." It is a clear message that this ancestral place orders the complex set of values that Wes carries as part of his memory of places. Work is only one aspect, of course; digging deeper still, we most likely would find many "values" that emanate from ancestral places and speak to the creation of individuals.

I decided . . . to focus on how Rockefeller might relate to something my father did very well—work with his hands. As part of a larger residential complex that I sketched, I thought about the workshop a man like Rockefeller might design and maintain for himself in a secluded estate. To begin this process, I remembered my father's workshop that existed in our garage: pegboard with tools hanging askance; oil stains; peach crates filled with bags of nails, screws, and bolts; great drums of grease for the farm equipment; odd containers my father had collected from the factory in which he worked; a great vise; and the like. I also recalled my effort as a child to straighten up my father's workbench once while he was away. I reorganized, cleaned, swept, hung, threw out, and later came to realize that the new order I had created actually concealed most of the tools, because I had moved them from where my father knew them to be.

The Rockefeller workshop sketches are influenced by my father, and by James Dine, Claus Oldenburg, and Julia Child as well. In the worlds

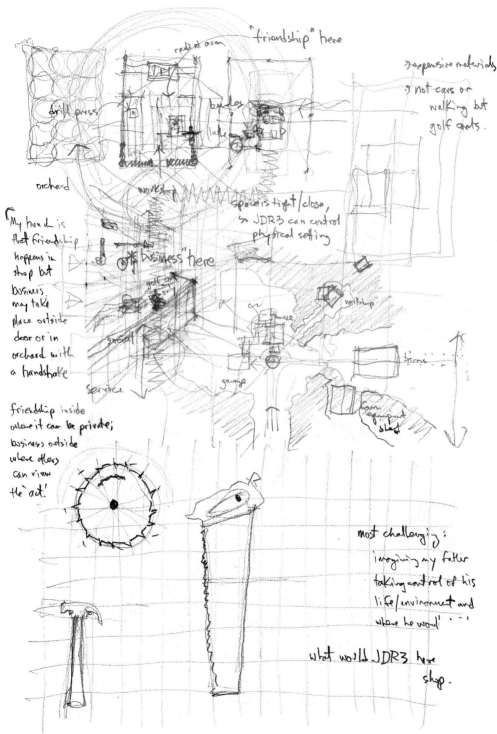

fig. 8. Workshop, by Wes Janz

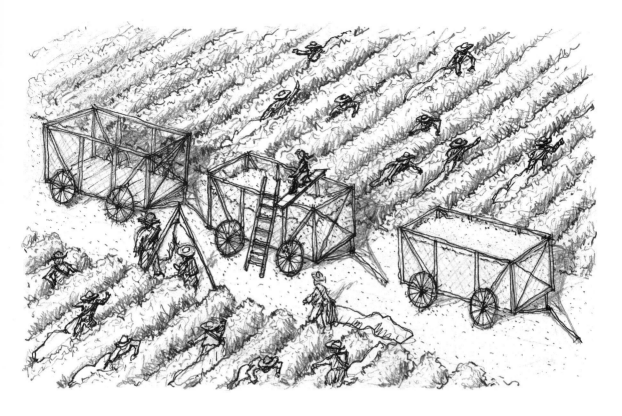

fig. 9. Cotton, by
Frances Downing

of these workers, our understandings of tools are challenged. Dine fabricates and contorts his own tools; Oldenburg makes tools out of assorted
materials and at megascales; Child—who presents herself as perfectly
organized in her pegboarded workshop—uses the most wonderfully made
devices to bring her great creations to life.

In the sketching exercise, I drew upon memories of my father, of
gallery exhibits done by Dine and Oldenburg, and of Child's WGBH
television show to visualize the hypothetical workshop of Rockefeller
3rd. The tools became dominant, essential, organized, clean, as does the
small building that is the workshop; clean lines, the pegboard grid enlarged to determine wall locations, the edges of benches, and the like.
(Wes Janz, appendix 3)

Places of Self

Another domain, similar in its attributes to ancestral places, reflects an empathic identification of self with place. *Places of self* begin to be identified

*Remembrance
and the
Design of Place*

32

during youth but continue to be named throughout young adulthood and maturity. All these places were event- and place-specific and therefore form one of the most basic structures of past, present, and future autobiographical knowledge. I remember the San Joaquin Valley as the "place" of my childhood. In the hot summer, the fields yielded rows of cotton. Trailers made of bright red metal frames and wire mesh would line one end of a field, waiting for their white pickings. The activity in the field consisted of people of many colors bent over the plants with long sacks of cotton dragging between their legs. I was so young that I was not expected actually to pick much cotton, so I brought each small gunny sack to the foreman, who would stoically weigh it, slight as it was, from a tripod contraption. Then I would climb the ladder to the top of the designated trailer and step out onto a board that was supported across the top of the trailer frame. Inching across the board to the middle, I would empty my gunny sack. When the foreman wasn't looking, I would jump into the cotton, burrow into this white world with its black, sharp seeds. This escape was short-lived, as the foreman could not allow such silliness too long. He could not be expected to indulge children in an event that was impossible for them to resist; the bed of cotton required each child to make this pilgrimage.

Mark Moreno identifies as a place of self the porch of his childhood home, a place where he can stand apart from his numerous brothers and sisters. His character for the game of Spatial Solitaire is himself, and he is engaged in the act of "flying." This proves an enlightening experience for the designer, as he delves into the meaning hidden behind this particular memorable place. A place that is "his" by occupation—away from the frenzy of complex family life, where one can be the protected daydreamer.[10] Places of self are valued most for their emotional content where there is very little distinction between place and person. Designers see some of their memorable places as empathetic experiences that serve as critical milestones in their self discoveries and seal their identities at certain periods of their lifetimes. Bedrooms, intimate dining places, complex and busy public spaces, cathedrals, chapels, meadows and broad views of the landscape can all induce self-oriented reflection and identification. There is no particular scale. Self-orientation can as easily involve looking out as looking in, intimacy or isolation, places that stretch to the horizon or places that enclose and protect.

The discovery came by taking this sketch as a challenge to revisit a memory which I feared would produce unknown evils. In the process, it became evident and significant that I was always alone in my memories of the porch. This is ironic, because I have seven brothers and sisters,

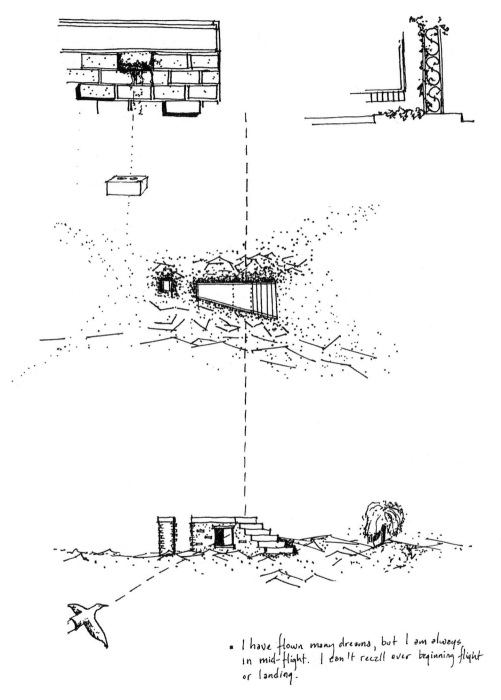

. I have flown many dreams, but I am always in mid-flight. I can't recall ever beginning flight or landing.

fig. 10. Front Porch, by Mark Moreno

34

and the house was relatively small. I discovered that part of my identity lay in the meaning of the porch, for, as soon as I opened the door, I would cease to be an individual. The porch consequently always represents a place of security. It gives me the ability, the confidence, and the freedom to distinguish myself from my siblings. (Mark Moreno, appendix 4)

Places of Self are inescapably connected to *moments of being*[11] because of the implication that discovery, reflection, and realization are personal self-oriented revelations. For designers, these moments of being often are intimately tied to particular places or journeys. The attributes of these kinds of places are complex and varied but all share a sense of strong physical identity and sensuousness. Places of strong light or deep shadow, places that are soft or hard, textured or smooth—it doesn't matter as long as it is strong, powerful, compelling, and identifying. These sensate characteristics mark the presence of "charged" energy or deep quiet.

fig. 11. Wyoming, by Lori Ryker

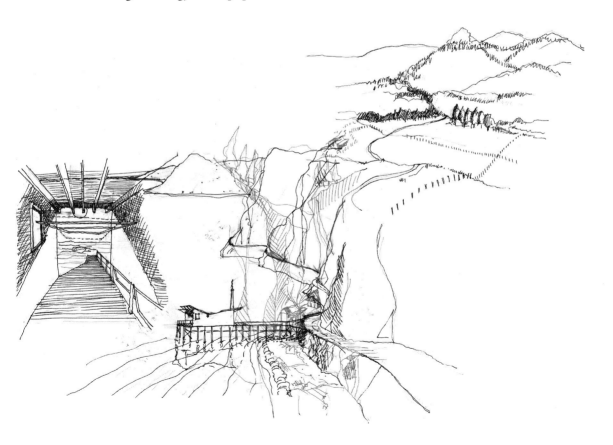

Lori Ryker's exercise in spatial solitaire also involves the domain of places of self in a characteristic moment of being. A significant part of her identity is tied to both a place and a person. The character is Gretel Ehrlich, whose act involves writing and ranching. The story is complex, but Lori's memory of a Cabin in Crazy Women Canyon provides a design direction for a place of contemplation and retreat for Gretel who needs to be "healed." Lori's identity *is* that of the vast Wyoming landscape—there she feel's whole, complete. She attempts to translate this sense of completeness to Gretel's place of recovery, contemplation, and retreat—in California.

> I fly a lot in my memories; I see better this way. I remember quality of light: sharp in the winter; smells: clean; warmth: in the winter sun; cold: in the snow. I hear voices: laughter; rushing water; snow crunching. I hear myself silent, breathing, watching, reflecting, wanting this place for my own. It is the degree to which I sense these things in Wyoming that I attempted to recover when I played [the game of Spatial Solitaire]. Not the building, or material or details, but the world engaged and bouncing upon my intentions in material. (Lori Ryker, appendix 5)

Sensate Places

In one of the most common domains, sensual experience—the extension of the body—is the pervasive characteristic of place. In *sensate places,* the body moves, sees, touches, smells, hears, and responds to the pleasure or pain of sensations. Such places heighten a particular sensation and create a strong identity based upon it: the smell of raisins in my grandmother's kitchen, the light streaming through a clerestory window in the cathedral at Toledo, the color and proliferation of tiles in an English church, the use of mirror reflections in Sir John Soane's house, the sweep of the roof at Ronchamp, the taste of ouzo in a Turkish bar. This domain begins to take on objective, analytical importance during the years of education and remains a universal reference for professional designers. Sensate places are powerful contents of memory and are transferred to the design of future places more easily than memories in some other domains.

Donna Kacmar, whose character is a woman in the act of bathing, suggests that the sensate memory is one charged with the whole range of possible sensations—warmth, aroma, texture, sound, and light. These sensations permeate the image and titillate us, arousing our own memories of such experiences. The sensual nature of places is designers' experiential bread and butter; sensory experience is what they cast forward into the void of design. The immediacy of all senses is heightened by such memories, allowing the designer to hold experiential sensations of place for a limited time of contemplation. Designers whom I interviewed often tried to express a sense of light that penetrates space. They often referred to the "shape" of light or the "color" of experience—mixing modes of experience to try to get at its richness and suspend the experience for moments in time, defining a possible future.

The act of drawing the plan of the bathroom begins to suggest a hierarchy of elements. There is the vessel or tub. A heat source—the radiator. A window allows air, light, and sound to enter from the street below. Another provider of water—the sink. There are the inhabitants, the bather and the observer.

The window. It is high and opens up completely. Other windows from other rooms are remembered and revisited. Looking down from above, being in the safety and seclusion of a raised room. Other tubs and water vessels are recalled.

fig. 12. Bathing Room, by Donna Kacmar

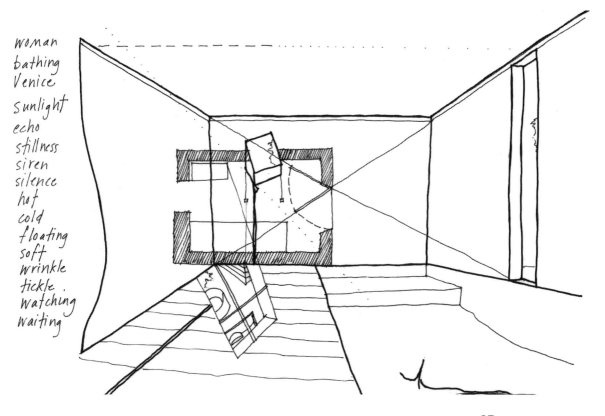

woman
bathing
Venice
sunlight
echo
stillness
siren
silence
hot
cold
floating
soft
wrinkle
tickle
watching
waiting

From the layout of the original memory, the essential pieces suggest future alignments and extensions. The layout of the new space is determined in part by the devices of memory. (Donna Kacmar, appendix 6)

The body and all its extensions into place, its ability to record movement, smell, touch, taste, sound and light for our consciousness and our memories, are among the most powerful tools for design. To imagine the body/self in place is the only way architects can practice their profession. Without this key domain, the numerous sensual places of our existence, we would be bereft of the pleasure we take in our bodies' recording of experience, our desire to recreate remembered existence. Often that desire is the clearest message we receive from the past.

Mary Silveria, in her essay for the game Spatial Solitaire, describes important sensate images that she gathered from Wisconsin and mingled with a cacophony of sounds, textures, and experiences from East Coast beaches and numerous other sites. Designed for Walt Whitman with emotion and sensation, the stroll is to be a place of change, of cycles, each with its own beauty. The path is a manifestation of these experiences: "Through nature we sense peace, an understanding of the way things are. Our emotions are affected by the time of the year and the moment in the day. The objective is to create space that accepts the natural order of change." More specifically:

Change of seasons.
The transformation of nature throughout the year.
The changes of color, light—visual.
The changes of temperature—sensual.

- Memories of stark, white, skeletal birches in winter.
- Memories of budding wildflowers, newborn birds, raging waters in spring.
- Memories of bright sunny skies, parched underbrush, ripe blueberries in summer.
- Memories of reds, yellows, browns, and greens in autumn.

All are a part of the cycle of nature, the cycle of life.
My life.
Walt's life. (Mary Silveria, appendix 7)

Places of Desire

Beginning in young adulthood and continuing into maturity, image banks include places of desire. These tend to be associated with private experiences,

though not exclusively. Places shared by lovers are remembered as physical desire, where sensation and emotion are intertwined: the color of a room, the quality of light, a breeze blowing softly through a window.

For the game of Spatial Solitaire, Jim Asbel creates the character Miss Endicott and, perhaps, a former lover. From movies featuring American soldiers in Britain during World War II and the powerful, often brief love affairs played out in British boardinghouses, with their shared bathrooms and front hall telephones, the former "friend" imagines Miss Endicott's present life in London. Boardinghouses in old movies always seem to juxtapose a staircase with the hall phone. The comings and goings of characters—their secret desires, their secret lives—develop a set of vicarious relationships that tease the boundary between *places of desire* and *sensuous places*.

fig. 13. A Stroll, by Mary Silveria

*Domains of
Place Experience*

39

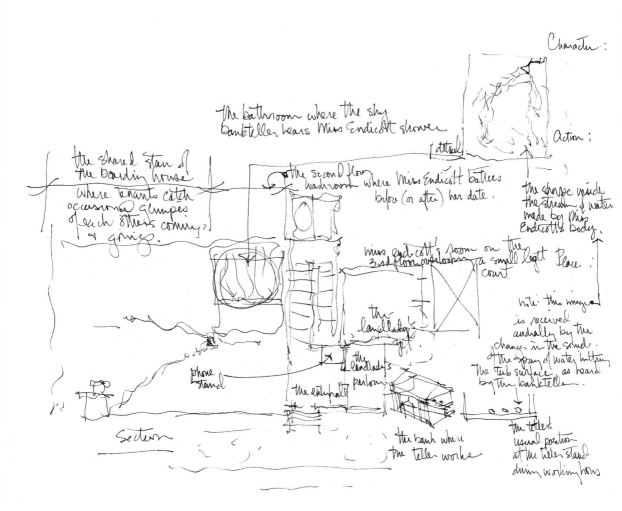

Character:

Action:

The bathroom where the shy
bankteller hears Miss Endicott shower

the shared stair of
the boarding house
where tenants catch
occasional glimpses
of each others' comings
& goings.

the second floor
washroom where Miss Endicott bathes
before (or after) her date.

[attic]

the change inside
the stream of water
made by Miss
Endicott's body.

Miss Endicott's room on the
3rd floor overlooks a small light
court

Place:

note: this image
is received
aurally by the
changes in the sound
of the spray of water hitting
the tub surface as heard
by the bankteller.

the
landlady's
apt

phone
stand

the
landlady's
parlour

the entryhall

the bank where
the teller works

the teller's
usual position
at the teller stand
during working hours

Section

fig. 14. Miss Endicott,
by Jim Asbel

*Remembrance
and the
Design of Place*

Character: Miss Endicott, a long-lost friend, has gone off to London,
where, residing in a boardinghouse, she remains out of touch
with her anxious friends back home.

Action: Miss Endicott is called to the phone in the entry hall by a
fellow boarder (a balding bank teller). She hears and considers the question of the caller's identity. She prepares to
descend the staircase.

The staircase is only imagined by an anxious friend back home. It is an
imaginative reconstruction from several period movies about U.S. servicemen dating young British girls during World War II. Upon this synthetic
space are superimposed auditory and tactile sensations derived from staircases actually experienced by this friend. It is not the friend, by the way,

40

who is calling on the phone. The friend, who in fact is imagining the entire scene, speculates that the caller is perhaps a new lover with whom Miss Endicott has become totally obsessed. (Jim Asbel, appendix 8)

The intimacy of desire is referenced by, and emotionally necessary to, design professionals. This domain manifests itself in the strong and compelling drive to capture a sense of being or "returning" that can be remembered but sometimes is lost to current experience. We all sense its presence in design but are hard pressed to express it in language. Often this recognition will take the form of admiring design talent that reflects professional, physical, or objective desire for inspiration. This recognition can express itself as a kind of question: "How do I reach this level of elegance (competence, finish, etc.)?" Physically, we recognize the influence of this domain in design through a feeling of missing something important, as much as through admiration for someone else's work. Objective admiration also can be a true respect for talent and a desire to understand and create beautiful, compelling places. Places of desire share a complicated mixture of pleasure, hope, and discretion.

Steven Moore grasps the central concept here: "Having made many architectural pilgrimages in my life, I have experienced a few exemplars with enough intensity to produce lasting subjective memories. Five days of house-sitting at Wright's Fallingwater, for example, left a vivid memory of the hand-hewn stone floors at my feet, not in my visual stockpile of design 'moves'" (appendix 16).

Places of Comfort

Also beginning with youth and extending into adulthood, places of comfort can be either emotional responses to places where the person is "comforted" or experiential places that are qualitatively "comfortable." These places range in scale from overstuffed chairs or the space under the stairs to an intimate forest or cars moving through the landscape. They tend to be characterized by small size, physical properties like softness, or a quality of light. At other times, these places are categorized by the presence of people, such as lovers, friends, or family, or by such activities as eating Thanksgiving dinner or playing cards. The only attribute shared across all these varied experiences is intimacy—sometimes the kind of intimacy that involves the presence of others.

Vince Canizaro has an unusual character, or pair of characters, for Spatial Solitaire. The act is to design a dog house; the designer is Curious George, and the client is Vince's dog. Vince recalls a series of places, all favorites—a design studio, a house in Seattle, and a house in New York. Comfort is a

Domains of Place Experience

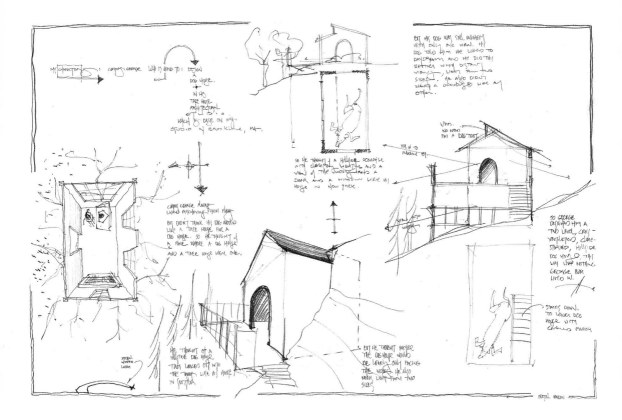

common theme, one that recalls our most cherished places from adulthood. The results of my research seem to indicate that "comfort" is intertwined with many of the other domains, but that its understanding as an essence emerges in adulthood. This does not mean that, as children, we did not find "comfort" in some of the places we name as memorable. Rather, I think children have less concern with the objective of comfort, and their experiences are more "emotional" and fantastic. Comfort seems to be a domain of adults; yet, as adults remember childhood experiences, they can categorize some of them as "comfortable" and describe why they were so.

Remembrance and the Design of Place

"In considering a place to begin," says Vince Canizaro, "I thought back to my favorite design-studio space, which was a second-story single room, much like what I depicted in the drawing. This memory spurred me forward to consider schemes for the dog house as emerging from desirable places in my past: my house in Seattle which faced a ravine, my house in New York which provided the notion of clerestory windows and glass walls, and other micro place memories, which come in tidbits during designing and thinking" (appendix 9).

42

Gregarious Places

A social domain closely linked to places of activity or participation (see below) consists of places responding to the desire of individuals to connect. Gatherings at restaurants, clubs, family reunions, county fairs, student unions, baseball games, and theaters are the types of place experiences generally assigned to the domain of *gregarious places*. Although shared places comprise a domain similar to this one, in terms of the functional realms of places named, shared places need not be particularly gregarious. The basic functional realm that relates the two domains is one of contact—the desire of members of our species to relate to one another, to not have to face the world alone, to be surrounded by others, to commune.

Robert Vickery, a designer who participated in this study, describes the kind of gregarious experience that opposes his initial memory. He uses Frank Lloyd Wright's house design at Fallingwater as a model for a "burger joint" on the Pennsylvania Turnpike. Fallingwater is a formal memory, either remembered as a first-hand experience or as a vicarious memory drawn from publications—a kind of icon for many designers. The house is a vacation house that communes with its landscape and which originally served as a family retreat with invited guests. One can imagine a life of ease, centered on enjoyment of the surrounding site. Vickery's use of Fallingwater as the basis for a commercial design on a turnpike seems to have to do with its active and dynamic structure of cantilevers and balconies. These serve as overlooks and potential places for communing either with others or the landscape (including, in Robert's imagination, the open highway). This becomes an active place, with neon and busloads of people taking advantage of its push-and-pull characteristics.

Places of Region

This domain is interwoven in complex ways with *places of topography,* or *places of geography,* for all are described to similar purposes. *Places of region* have "identity"; they speak to designers in a language of tradition. Place memories often are tied to a larger network of connections to the land, to townscapes or cityscapes, and to the choreography of journey. This domain is a domain not of "type" but rather of an identity. Place is strongly identified by its ecoregion, the prevailing images of landscape, merged with myth and tradition.

Ed Burian speaks to this domain, as his essay describes what it is to design in the American Southwest. He describes the evolution of ideas as

Domains of Place Experience

43

F3 (Transformation)

uncle Frank's

To Pittsburgh

"The Best Burgers in Pennsylvania" at Uncle Frank's Restaurant.

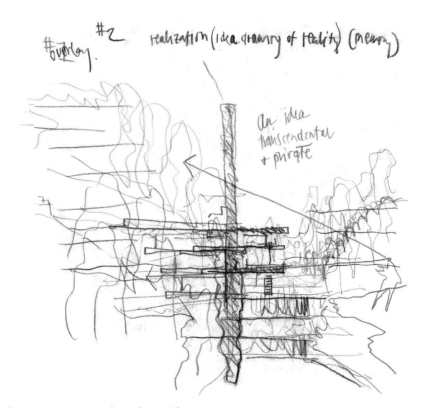

#overlay. #2   realization (idea drawing of reality) (memory)

an idea
transcendental
+ private

fig. 16. Burger Joint, by Robert Vickery

44

they relate to an actual design project, rather than a game of Spatial Solitude. There is more than one theme, of course, but the one we are interested in here is Ed's concern for the region and how that concern is identified with a "new" addition to the Sonoran Desert. The mix of vernacular organization on site and modern compositional manipulation describe a juncture at which regional identity meets specific site, function, and clients. In addition to regional identity, Burian is concerned with what we might call *places of inflection*—there is a "language" of materials and detail that are appropriate to a place. This intonation of place and site is found in many architectural projects. For many professionals and students, materials and their use—the language of a particular place and that place's identity with its regional place— are significant beginnings for design.

This residence intentionally engages the ambiguity which constitutes our daily experience of place in a postindustrial age in the American Southwest. Our experience of the Southwest and its meaning is formed both by the direct experience of the desert landscape, with its numerous sensuous qualities; and by representations of the Southwest and Mexico in films, literature, and television. True, the residence intentionally recollects memories of traditional vernacular building types in the Sonoran Desert, such as haciendas, ranches, and courtyard buildings . . . in terms of its organization on the site, traditional articulated transitions from public to private domains, and outdoor circulation under covered arcades . . . Even so, it utilizes compositional strategies from modern architecture, such as the interpenetration of exterior and interior space, and makes use of the possibilities of building with the materials and electronic technologies of our time. (Ed Burian, appendix 10)

Vicarious Places

During their years of professional education, young designers tend to shift their memorable imagery from informal to more formal place imagery— that is, to places that are "designed" and therefore formally recognized as examples of various periods of architectural development, or as belonging to the work of a known architect. These fall into the domain of *vicarious experience* and *admired architecture.* Typically, these images are acquired through books, journals, lectures, and related coursework. Some students travel during their years of education, generally exploring the admired architecture presented to them as part of their formal education. Examples most commonly mentioned are Ronchamp, Villa Savoye, Fallingwater (as in Robert

Domains of Place Experience

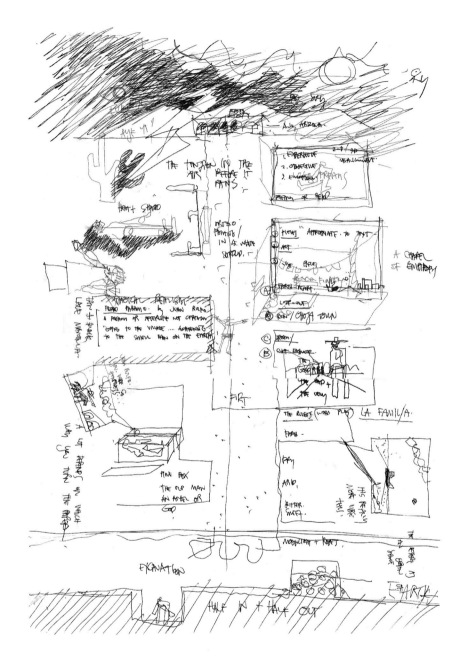

fig. 17. The Southwest, by Ed Burian, Architect

Vickery's use of Fallingwater as a precedent for a burger joint on an expressway), and other famous built forms, as well as emerging American and European designers (often those touted in journals), American and European cityscapes, and architecture local to the place of professional education. This period also introduces the young designer to a more analytical evaluation of

46

fig. 18. Drawing/
Etching/Seeing/
Mapping, by
Scott Wall

places, including principles of form, space, order, and behavior. While "informal" places also are experienced during this period, I have assumed that, given the tendency to introduce relatively abstract principles during education, young designers tend to apply a new vocabulary and set of principles to most places they encounter, interpreting them in terms of somewhat formal abstractions.

Scott Wall's use of the drawings of Piranesi is a clear example of a designer utilizing his imagination to explore, vicariously, the two-dimensional space of endless complication—spaces that turn into themselves and return again. Wall's struggle leads him to further references that are not particularly "architectural" in the sense of built form, but whose structures reinforce the original search. Scott applies these ideas to an imagined place in Houston that is in need of complexity and duplicity.

*Domains of
Place Experience*

Since I first saw Giovanni Battista Piranesi's Carceri d'Invenzione in 1980, I have remembered and drawn and tried to understand the chiaroscuro depths of those incomprehensible spaces, mapping and recording the associative power of those precursors of modernism. Over and over, I sink into the map and the memory—obsessively, through and across and within time—to this momentary present in which I write and try to remember a conflation of memories into one drawing.

And this drawing is of a room in Houston, which is not a room but the underbelly of the suburb: the relentless concrete of the freeway. This is a drawing of walls which are not walls, or of continuously reconfigured containers which will become wall-like, where memories of all of these figures, events, experiences have become a search through light and shadow for Piranesi's ghost. (Scott W. Wall, appendix II)

Abstract Places

Five additional domains emerged as results of the educational influence of abstract analysis. *Place types, schematic configurations, properties of places, rational/geometric exercises,* and *scripted behavior* are domains that evolved from educating students in the practice of analysis of place experience or *vicarious places.* These domains present more objective characteristics that prove useful during design and generally are devoid of emotional or experiential content when thought of analytically. These objective, abstract domains continue to be present for professionals during the years of practice. *Abstract,* for our purposes, is abstraction as defined by Susanne Langer: "the consideration of a form apart from any contents."[12] She stretches the meaning of "form" beyond its common connotation of shape, to include anything that may be said to follow a pattern or structure of any sort. This extended definition allows such things as music, ritual, or etiquette to have form. In abstraction, it is the *logical* form or structure that interests us, rather than a particular medium or, in this case, a particular place experience. These domains are schematic and are made from repeated occurrences with "like" conditions. Their accumulation in the designer's mind forces their individual locations to be lost in space and time.[13] The surroundings for these experiences have faded into the background but can be retrieved when the need arises. Although these abstract domains had little meaning for designers during their youth, mental images that emerge from childhood easily can be analyzed and located within them after the concepts of space, form, order, and behavior are introduced during the years of education.

Place types are places abstracted and linked together as a group, class, or taxonomy by shared attributes, rules of formation, or cultural manifestation. Most places belong to a "type," but some types are more prevalent than others. Buildings, vehicles, and tools, for example, generally display characteristics in common with their prototypes. *Type* presents to consciousness an abstract domain that, according to Aldo Rossi, is the architecture to which "life" is grafted. In this sense, Langer's reference to "functional realms" is a definition of "type" that Aldo Rossi most likely would appreciate. Typologies constitute generic images repeated over and over and attached to some common functional realm (schools, post offices, storefronts, houses, and so on). It is precisely the repetition of occurrences[14] that distinguishes a place type, rather than the more specific attributes that define other domains. For example, tree houses form a place type when they follow a generalized set of rules. They must be raised above the ground, but the distance is not a set one. They must somehow be attached to, or intimately juxtaposed with, trees. They range from a few boards awkwardly placed by small hands to elaborate and sophisticated platforms. Their reference as a *secret place,* on the other hand, depends on something specific—namely, the degree of shelter attained and limited accessibility.

Designers often make reference to a place type during design inquiry, without needing or desiring a particular manifestation. In many cases, a "type" is intimately known through its recurring manifestations in the history of built form. Ed Burian makes such a reference in his design of the house in the American Southwest (see appendix 10). He uses a "type" of courtyard house that is well known to him, so no specific place is called to our attention. It is understood that there is a pattern in this "type" and that its organization can be considered apart from any specific place within the hot, dry regions of the Southwest. Typologies are important to designers, because they represent a social contract between society and those who design and build. This contract declares that certain building types are resistant to unwelcome or inappropriate "change"—that is, change beyond specific site and environmental conditions that may impact the "type" and alter it slightly within its logical format.

Schematic configurations refer to a person's understanding of forms that are manifested in different types of places, events, or behaviors. Schematic configurations, while originally based in experience, become independent of images of place, existing as mental concepts that present diagrammatic and objective schematic images devoid of emotional or experiential content. Common generalizations like "axis down the middle" or "gathering in a circle for discussion" are examples of schematic configurations. These concepts are based in experience but have become so abstract as actions or spatial responses that they can exist as independent conceptions. The logical forms of these schematics vary, depending on function, like gathering, or on even more abstract aesthetics, like the golden section. Designers sometimes work

49

from a diagram called a *parti*. It is generally an abstract organizational schematic that may combine several schematic configurations.

For Thomas Carlson-Reddig, the axes in play are activated by a specific image of Saint Petersburg but also are repeated authoritatively all over the world. "Axis down the middle" becomes a symbol of formality and procession. It seems culturally pervasive, but in Western tradition it presents itself with a history of use that is beyond memory.

> The memory of places has played a significant role in the way I approach design. Such memory can be applied literally, as in the design of a residential college in the Appalachian Mountains, where we intentionally attempted to recall the way the Italian hill town responds to its setting; but most often the remembrances are not so easily translated.
>
> What I think is most important about remembering Saint Petersburg, through my own experience and through the writings of Dostoevski, is that the memories are rooted in a series of events and places rather than in a specific building or place. The connection of experiences, places, and events overwhelms the particular.
>
> The notion of how one experiences places is something I have tried to bring to all projects that I am involved with, whether it be an urban project or a small-scale building. (Thomas Carlson-Reddig, appendix 12)

The concept *properties of place* is similar to *schematic configuration* but often includes a measure of experiential content. Properties are named and objectified: large or small, round or square, up or down, crowded or deserted, open or closed, and so on. *Properties of place* are recounted by designers as external to self. While these manifestations are grounded in specific place experience, they become terms that objectify and analyze place in an intellectual mode rather than an experiential or emotional one. They entail naming characteristics or traits, singular or multiple, that are first experienced by the body and then conceptualized via dispassionate reasoning as conditions that objectively describe the physical features or list the qualities of places.

Rational/geometric exercises include images in which what is presented to the mind is some kind of system—a system of geometry, mathematics, ratios, or proportions that is drawn from the ability abstractly to manipulate from a numerical basis and create space within a set of rules that are bounded by the potential within the system. These are not specifically mental images from memory, although known structures can be analyzed through these techniques. Rather, this represents a bias towards immediate order, which

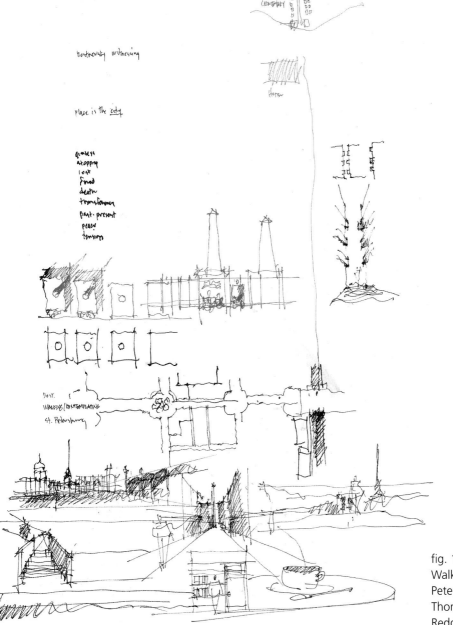

fig. 19. Dostoevski Walking in Saint Petersburg, by Thomas Carlson-Reddig

any system provides. It is useful in design, because the designer can organize the parts of a project systematically, giving the project an immediate geometric harmony that might be tested against programming requirements. Jef7rey Hildner's response to the Spatial Solitaire game displays some desire for a formal response through law-bound relations that lead to meaningful

51

associations. The memory has to do with a series of proportions/calculations that are tied to a number of artists and theorists. His drawing displays this abstract beginning. However, as moves are made in response to the design of an observatory, the relationship of proportions becomes rational (as a matter of fact) and intentional (as a matter of implication).

Move | Meaning (Form | Content)
Dialectical signifiers of a built project: *Dante | Telescope House*^{Zlowe}

Abstract Form

Painters	Diebenkorn, Gris, Mondrian, Léger, Radice
	$y = ax^2 + b + 18$ (Georges Vantongerloo, 1930)
Numbers 1:4:9:16|	"Creations of calculation . . . a superior
	mathematical order" (Le Corbusier, Terragni)
	(Jef7rey Hildner, appendix 13)

fig. 20. Fact and Implication, by Jef7rey Hildner

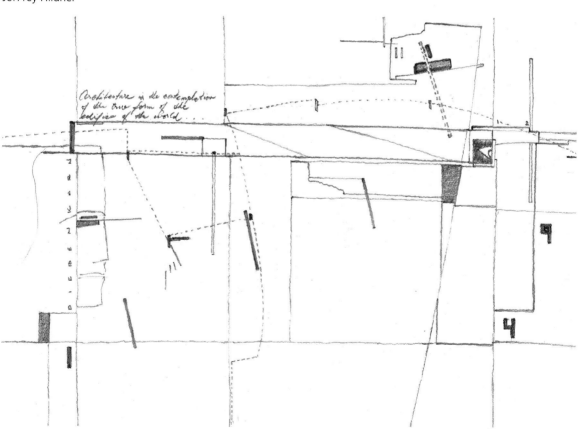

52

Similar in its abstraction, *scripted behavior* is present in the mind as schematic "scripts" for expected comportment in familiar situations. The scripts include abstracted understandings of appropriate, expected behavior dictated by cultural and societal norms. These experiences can range from the ritual behavior expected at weddings to common occurrences like eating a meal in a restaurant. Each step of the ritual or activity can be described in a linear fashion, in sequential steps that most people in a particular society accept as rational, anticipated, and probable behavior. Behavior that falls outside the expected norm particularizes the experience in some improvisational way. *Scripted behavior* is rehearsed by designers as they constantly "walk through" their paper architecture.[15] It is presumed behavior within clear functional realms. It is a conceptual abstraction in which "these kinds of behaviors" occur.

> However, these activities are reinterpreted in terms of contemporary culture. Covered places to sit outside and observe the landscape also include computer and video connections, while an outdoor bar to make margaritas and lemonade is situated adjacent to a lime and lemon grove.
>
> Directions are acknowledged in the residence and respond to both ancient and contemporary rituals. Bathing, cleansing, and a breakfast area are oriented to the east; a dining terrace for watching sunsets faces west; and the lights of daily commuters in their automobiles and city lights may be observed to the south in the evening. (Ed Burian, appendix 10)

FLUID DOMAINS

It is possible for a memorable place experience to range across the different domains identified here, depending upon the particular circumstances of design inquiry, seemingly unrelated intellectual activity, or serendipity. Instead of each place experience residing in one domain, there exists in memory a fluidity that identifies domains as temporary "hooks" (functional realms) upon which a specific place or event experience can be hung (understood in a particular light) for a period of time. When necessary, the same experience might be reformulated and understood through a different functional realm and hung from a different hook. Each image is fluid, because our memories are reconstructed through different filters and for different purposes as time and situation dictate.

Students seem to be caught in a formalized and generally analytical mode during their years of education.[16] Young students and even students who

*Domains of
Place Experience*

53

have completed most of their professional studies tend to create a boundary between the informal, memorable places of their youth and the formal, memorable places introduced to them during their years of education. While all the domains—secret places, ancestral places, Arcadian places, places of self, moments of being, sensate places, places of comfort, places of desire, gregarious places, places of activity, places of participation, shared places, vicarious experience, admired architecture, place types, schematic configurations, properties of place, rational/geometric exercises, and scripted behavior—were created and generally recounted by students and professionals alike, students found it difficult to conceptualize an informal image like grandmother's kitchen within the same domain as a formal image like Ronchamp. Students split their experiences of place into two distinct lifetime periods—before entering design education and after entering design education. This is not, of course, a surprising response. While students identified the same domains and similar categories as professionals, they generally put formal and informal places in different categories, whereas professionals mixed them across the themes they invented. Design education, therefore, seems to act as a very defined and structured boundary in a beginning designer's experience.

Researchers in the field of autobiographical memory have deduced that individuals orient their memories to lifetime periods that present different existential problems and life "themes." These periods are often associated with "life tasks" that comprise period-specific problems.[17] I would name four distinct periods in a designer's lifetime: (1) childhood, a period of socialization, of seeking an identity based in surrounding people, places, and experience; (2) the college years, a period of initiation during which individuals are presented with defined themes and face the difficulties of adding formal architectural imagery to the informal place imagery they accumulated during childhood; (3) the first ten years or so after college, a different level of initiation during which themes are elaborated, refined, or forgotten; and (4) the period in which mature designers and professional architects find a balance in which their themes are not strictly categorized according to formal and informal boundaries, but take on more existential qualities.

These boundaries disappear as memorable images are potentially aligned with varying domains. All domains are present to professional and student designers alike, and all domains are recognized as significant. The mature professional designer, however, displays a significantly greater fluidity than most students. This fluidity means that the "life" each image presents stretches across the formal/informal boundary, rendering that boundary irrelevant as professionals relate past place experiences to the potential places taking shape in their minds or on their drawing boards.

The typical architect's process of thinking about the nature of places matures beyond the principles which she or he may have acquired during the years of education. Years of practice add a range of formal and informal place imagery to the mature designer's memorable experiences. These experiences range from coffee houses, marketplaces, favorite haunts, and open landscapes to the high architecture of cathedrals or villas, recognized masterpieces, places designed by colleagues, and personal explorations in design. Mature designers no longer recognize any significant difference between the informal imagery of youth and the more formal imagery gained during and after education. Their sorting actions tell a story of seeing past this unfortunate division. The split image bank is fused into a fluid whole, where the source (formal or informal) of design imagery is of no importance when significance is the question.

The reasons for the disparity between students and professionals across commonly held domains undoubtedly are complex. Upon commencing their professional education, architecture students immediately and mercilessly are bombarded, as they should be, with place imagery from high architecture. Even if more vernacular examples are used, students are taught a very formal vocabulary of evaluation and application. None of this activity is wrong, but it may be incomplete. After all, schools of architecture are established to teach principles of form, space, order, and behavior, and to acquaint students with what most people consider important architecture. It is not often, however, that an instructor takes his or her students aside to remind them that they already possess a powerful bank of place experiences. Whether or not they know this, students generally are not taught how to "deal" with these unruly, ragged sets of places that cling to them, no matter what their education. If they pay any attention to them at all, most likely they try to approach a place image like grandmother's kitchen with the formal vocabulary and analytic skills usually applied to high architecture. This is generally unsatisfactory, because these formal vocabularies usually are devoid of emotional or experiential content. In the mature designer's mind, however, the "life" that the memorable images of places convey (contact, retreat, participation, identity, love, grace, sensuousness, intellect, intimacy, growth, expansiveness, reflection, communion), their overlapping domains, and their usefulness in particular design projects somehow converge. How the designer assimilates meaning, establishes domains, and uses memorable experience in design is the subject of the remainder of this book.

Domains of
Place Experience

55

Obviously, both the sorting technique used to establish domains and the remaining aspects of this research presuppose that categorization is basic to human mental operations. It is true that memory is inexact, never replicative, always open and dynamic. Memory is based, however, on association and generalization.[18] The mind is a growing and evolving entity, always in process, always processing. While categorizations and generalizations are important parts of this process, these activities never are closed or severely bounded. Instead, categories grow and change as the designer sifts more and more information from life experience and is influenced by "others."

Indeed, the physical mappings of the brain itself—the synaptic avenues of electrical firings—vary even among individuals (such as twins) who face seemingly identical environmental conditions. The brain must be able to order, however temporarily, incoming information from events and embodied experiences. Initially, the only order is sequence. This, however, proves inadequate except when lifespan "periods" are important. Temporal order tends to lose ground to mental constructions and time-of-life episodes that fit the patterns of experience. Even these categorizations always are in flux, because incoming information and experience require that the borders between categorizations be "fuzzy" and "loose," adjusting and readjusting through time. Domains, then, represent the functional realms of existing categorizations, but recollected memories are so complex that they can be reformulated to fit several domains.

"Memory is the great organizer of consciousness," Susanne Langer wrote.[19] This capacity to frame relationships, or to categorize experience, is a capability humans developed even before they developed language. Perceptual categorization is a capacity we share with other animals. It is unconscious and automatic. Conceptual categorization, however, requires both perceptual categorization *and* memory, and gives rise to scenes or images. According to Edelman, perceptual categorizations (those whose source is outside the body) and conceptual categorizations (those whose source is inside the mind) are based in primary consciousness. Primary consciousness is the kind of consciousness that, to different degrees, we share with other creatures. Primary consciousness, however, always is constrained by the tyranny of the present, a here-and-now that can be broken only by the development of a higher order of consciousness—a symbolic memory.[20]

Remembrance
and the
Design of Place

Our capacity for speech and symbolic expression shows that we are conscious to a higher degree than other animals. We have evolved special brain structures and concurrent physical structures that permit these behaviors.

We are conscious of being, whether that involves a true self, a social self, or measures of each. Meanwhile, symbols present our memory with associated meaning. Without symbol-making activity, we would be unable to construct a socially based selfhood or a model of the world in terms of past and future. We could not be directly aware of things not present. Symbolic memory, then, and the development of communication (words, drawings, dance, story telling, and so on), through our ability to elaborate, refine, connect, and create, sets us apart from most other creatures.[21]

The ability to categorize suggests that, while meaning resides in the significance we place on the concepts we derive from repeated experience, growth and changing values require a "process" whereby adjustment occurs. Both hard-core research and philosophy lead to the same conclusion: the basic process of change, or even thought, is fundamentally metaphoric in nature. Humans juxtapose present experience with past experiences that have formed prototypical and resemblance references. This kind of referencing is an evolutionary, biological function of human minds. Continuous referencing leads to the creation of a *gestalt*, a complex of separate properties that, when taken together, are basic to human experience. We "create" our experience through active and dynamic perceptual generalizations, concept formations, and memory—an unstoppable orchestration of the mind.[22]

Categorization requires memory. Dynamic changes in the mapping of connections in our brains means that evolving categories are derived from memory through a process of analogic and metaphoric reference. Analogic comparisons are those involving referents that are more similar to each other than dissimilar. Metaphoric comparisons are those involving referents that are more dissimilar to each other than similar.[23] With analogic reference, a category can change, but the change would be minimal because the new experience generally "fits" within an existing category. The new experience may cause a "shifting" of value rather than any significant change, or it may simply reinforce the existing value of a category. Our open-ended environment, however, sometimes requires a radical recategorization, one that can be accommodated only by metaphoric reference. The difference between analogic and metaphoric reference, then, is defined here as one of range. It can be visualized as a continuum. Comparisons of new experience with old can fall anywhere along this continuum. At one end, very little shifting of concepts is necessary, and analogic reference is sufficient. On the other end, an upheaval of categories, requiring recategorization and metaphoric reference, is required.

Chapter 3

Significant Form of Memorable Place

A THEORY OF MEMORY and imagination in design must rise from the practice of architecture and the process by which a designer makes virtual and actual places. To begin with abstract theories of language, apart from an experiential base, is misleading and lifeless. The emotional, experiential, and intellectual content of our experiences; our ability to transform an unknown design task into a knowable resolution; the transfer of meaning to future places; our capacity for adjustment and fit—all these things must be understood in light of what we know about the importance of past place experience and its impact on design. This process of reference also implies that we value some categories more than others, as we continuously reinforce synaptic connections in the brain (these connections physically grow larger and provide sturdy, physical mappings) because they link symbolic and semantic abilities.[1]

In rejecting abstract syntactical descriptions of mental operations and representations as a viable way of describing the designer at work, I must replace this explanation with one that is born out of researching how architects think and use past place experience. I am not proclaiming a formal, unifying explanatory theory; rather I am suggesting a more modest theory for understanding the natural weaving of memory with design. I begin with material collected from designers and employ two linked theories to help clarify a relationship between memory and imagination. I use Gerald Edelman's theory of evolution and selection to explain the *physical* workings of the mind. Edelman's theory of neural Darwinism is a highly pragmatic approach to theory building that draws on hard data from embryology, morphology, physiology, and psychology. At the same time, I use Susanne Langer's *Philosophy in a New Key* and her theory construction in *Feeling and Form* to explore a powerful "fit" between her ideas about human expression and the domains of place that I discovered in my own work. In addition to weaving neural Darwinism with Langer's theories of symbolic expression, I rely upon certain phenomenological doctrines to support my view of "connections" among ourselves as designers, the people for whom we design, and the fibers of meaning that thread through time.

There is still much understanding to be sifted from Edelman, Langer, and the phenomenologists. A significant criticism of this work is my effort to fold these very different world views into a coherent explanation of my research. Nevertheless, I feel it is necessary to introduce them after my findings have been discussed. This introduction represents my effort to draw the past and the future together in the present. Edelman's Pragmatic neural evolutionary theory and Langer's Neo-Structuralist or Symbolist approach at first glance do seem disparate; each author's presentation is unique in its forum. Yet both Edelman and Langer stray beyond the strict boundaries that mark the classical positions held by scholars who ostensibly share their world views. In some places, their theories overlap. It is precisely in these overlapping positions, these "in-betweens," that I find my material fits best.

A SHORT, SELECTIVE HISTORY OF THE MIND

The desire of Immanuel Kant (1724–1804) to mend the duality of objective and subjective worlds by constructing an ingenious view of the mind-body relationship is what produced our modern Western image of the range of the mind's workings. A strict Kantian view of the mind shifts from a conception of the mind as a receptacle for external stimuli to a conception of the mind as an active mediator between sensation and sense. The mind becomes an agent of order that structures ideas of nature. This capacity for ordering is shared by all humans and is not learned; rather, the human mind *a priori* possesses certain transcending "forms" that are universal. In this view, the world no longer is simply "out there" but is dependent upon our experience of it.[2] The world, in Kant's view, is idealistic—constituted out of ideas. The mind imposes structure upon the sensate world it encounters; and its knowledge of that world is basic to, yet independent of, experience. In this way, Kant balances the subjective (that which is inside the subject, the absolute, transcendental self) with the objective (that which is outside the subject and necessary to it).

Significant Form

The existence of transcending and universal characteristics of the mind suggests that culture, society, and cognition are only portions of the evolving "self." The transcendental self is universal, not personal or psychological. Underlying the dynamic individual is the human mind, with its controlling "forms" that tie each person to an encompassing network of humanity, despite superficial differences. Memories, therefore, are idiosyncratic versions of shared constructions of experience. Although culture, society, and specific experiences play a part in this development of the particular self, the transcendental self is absolute and independent of particular perspectives. After Kant, this image of a mind that binds subjective and objective reality diverges onto different paths, two of which are of interest here. One follows a phenomenological route, the other a constructivist route.

THE PHENOMENAL PATH

Edmund Husserl (1859–1938) posited a phenomenological standpoint that makes a distinction, like Kant's, between consciousness and its objects. Husserl suspended the natural standpoint (that all knowledge comes from experience) and suggested that one does not examine the *objects* of experience, but rather the *entire complex of the way we experience* objects, without regard to the actual existence of the objects themselves (objects can be ideas, constructs, memories). My grandmother's kitchen no longer exists as the object I once knew in an experiential, emotional, and intellectual sense. Husserl is implying that it is not the physical kitchen that is important here. Rather, it is my intentions toward the memory of this kitchen that are significant. It is "how" I remember, not "what" I remember, that is of interest. This position legitimizes mental imagery as phenomena worthy of study. The phenomenological standpoint seeks the *essence* of ideas that *present* themselves in experience. Like Kant, Husserl believed that timeless and objective structures exist in the mind, independent of particular perspectives. But for Husserl, the subjective was made of essential structures of consciousness, and the objects of consciousness consisted of intentional objects.[3] It is our *intentions* toward objects that constitute the subject matter of concern; they are the only "truth" that can be sought.

The search for essential structures was taken up by Martin Heidegger (1889–1976), who, unlike his mentor Husserl, or Kant, made no distinction between mind and body, or between consciousness and anything else. He called this unity Being-in-the-World. Heidegger suggested that it is being itself, rather than the existence of beings, that is in question; and that our *understanding* of being does not derive from our *knowledge* of particular things. The ontological result of this interest in the nature of our own being leads existential phenomenologists in a direction that may assist the designer in a very personal way, for this approach seeks to *work out,* rather than to *find out,* the essence of being. Its seductiveness lies in its raising of equipment, tools, and instruments *ready at hand* as the primary means of engagement with the

Remembrance and the Design of Place

world. What designers do naturally is *use* a bit of the world; knowledge often is the deep background for involvement. The world is organized according to one's task, and it is the understanding of this relationship that is the key to enlightenment. An existential-phenomenological world view is alluring to architectural designers because it infers that working in the world will lead to true in-sight. Designers who enjoy the handling of materials, the nature of tools, and the quality of work itself do well with this philosophy. However, it is not a philosophy that is "handy" in terms of explanation. For, unlike Husserl's brand of phenomenology, its goal is not explanation but understanding.

Phenomenology, for all its complexity, does move memory, mental imagery, and imagination to the forefront of its inquiries. Gaston Bachelard, a phenomenologist who dwells on *The Poetics of Space,* states, "Something closed must retain our memories while leaving them their original values as images."[4] Images, for Bachelard, transcend any one memory, although each individual image is concrete evidence for the transcending experience. As a child of California ranch life, I remember that the land was populated by very large and colorful beasts which plowed fields and masqueraded as machinery. In the early spring, the monster plows turned over about a foot of earth and left long furrows to dry in the sun. One of my brothers became especially proficient at building clod forts from the turned, dried earth. He sometimes allowed me to help build these enclosures. Probably they were no more than six by four feet—but, of course, they seemed much larger at the time. It was an act of enclosure and protection from a potentially threatening world (other ten- to twelve-year-old boys). From the forts that we built every spring, great battles were fought.

This specific memory of built enclosure and protection is transcending. All who have ever hidden behind the couch or on the fire escape, or built brush enclosures, have fought these same battles and waged valiant wars to protect and defend. Although Bachelard uses mental imagery as a vehicle for his philosophical musings, his goal, like that of all existential phenomenologists, is to *understand*, rather than *explain,* being. To analyze being in ontological terms, one would need to *desocialize* our important memories, to "know" primary history through primary images—those images which have their own history, their own life. I would utilize my particular forts and my particular brother to "understand" the desire to enclose, protect, and defend. Bachelard would judge these intentions to be "primary," in that all humans, no matter what their social or cultural identities, would hold the same intentions toward this memory because they too have experienced something very "like" it. It is essential to being human. This process of investigating the nature of being leads the phenomenologist to move beyond

Significant Form

61

the specific—what Bachelard refers to as the psychological—to the shared essences of experience.

To discover the nature of being, proponents of existential phenomenology claim, they must move beyond the rationalism of contemporary science and become receptive to the phenomenon in question. The "image" is a central phenomenon for most proponents of phenomenology, because it is already once removed from concrete experience. Its existence allows the initiate to "be" part of the actual world and to contemplate its existence more completely. The image, then, is less subject to positioning within a line of history; it has, instead, a life of its own.

Yet Bachelard admits to a "subjectivity" and a "transubjectivity"—personal experience of a poetic image and the ability of an image to transfer us beyond subjective involvement into a kind of connection with the nature of the image—that is, a realization of its essence. Both these states have potential for the act of design. The first, subjectivity, is primarily pragmatic. The second, transubjectivity, allows the elimination of its specific history and strives to connect particular images to others on a plane that is independent of idiosyncratic memory, though understood through it. The existential phenomenologist would transcend the need for the particular and the subjective; in fact, these mundane realities get in the way of discovering or realizing the significance of being. I maintain, however, as does Husserl's version of phenomenology, that, for any useful understanding of the essential, it is critical to revisit the particular (our idiosyncratic experience).

THE CONSTRUCTIVIST PATH

While phenomenology may prove to be a strong tool for understanding the essential nature of being, its resistance to explanation often leaves a residue of mysticism. Constructivism, on the other hand, maintains the Kantian position of a complementary mind-body composition of reality, while pursuing a more direct path to understanding. Its development has taken place mostly in connection with research in cognitive psychology. Like the anthropologist Levi-Strauss, many of its proponents do not begin with philosophy but are led back to philosophy by the need to explain the outcomes of their research. We need not provide a detailed review of the odd combinations of structuralism, pragmatism, dualism, and other "isms." Essentially, constructivism is a view that the mind/brain and the world construct each other.

Psychologist Frederick Bartlett in 1932 introduced the idea of "construction" as the process by which memory works. Bartlett posited that mental imagery had a central role in perception. According to Bartlett, the mind, rather than storing sensate information as it is perceived, stores essential, abstracted patterns—schemata—derived from experience. From these schemata, memorable images can be reconstructed. Bartlett's research was effectively quashed by behaviorism, the cognitive arm of positivism, and this constructivist view was held hostage until the cognitive psychologist Jean Piaget (1896–1980) began to publish his research.[5]

Kant suggested that the world supplies the *content* of knowledge (the sensations of the world), while the mind is structured to supply the *form* of knowledge (the ordering of experience). Kant's theory posits innate categories in the mind that are used to process knowledge of the world. If I were in my grandmother's kitchen, the *content* of my world would be smells, visual forms, warmth, etc. According to Kant, it would be the structure of my mind that would make it possible for me to "make sense" out of sensation. Some of the structures that Kant proposed to be innate to human understanding of sensation were cause and effect, unity, plurality or community, and necessity-contingency, among other "forms" through which we organize our experiences.

Piaget developed an alternative to the notion of innate "forms." He theorized that "the mind and the world mutually construct each other. That is, just as Kant had shown that the mind's schemata order and regulate information from the outside world, Piaget has tried to show how that information can also shape the schemata themselves."[6] In going beyond Kant's original premise, Piaget theorized that the internal schemata are developed and modified through external experience of the world. This would mean that my understanding of the reality of my grandmother's kitchen would be an evolving opera, unfolding as I matured and revisited the space, activities, and people; shaping its meaning as I progressed through time and memory. Piaget also theorized that the process of developing schemata follows a course of assimilation and accommodation. The human capacities for assimilation and accommodation are innate structures of the human mind.

Assimilation, for Piaget, is a process of discovery, the organic ability by which humans order complex new experience. A developing individual is seen as a *tabula rasa;* the human meets challenges in the world by developing schemata to match the problems encountered, building a repertoire of behavioral referents, scripts, and maps. Once a repertoire of referents has been built in the individual's mind, any new experience in the world is recognized analogically through comparison to similar, already-known referents. The assimilation of experience through schematic match is posited as basic cognitive development. I would compare all new kitchen experiences with those I had stored in my original encounters. They would be recognized as a simi-

Significant Form

lar "kind" of experience, one that I would recognize and through which I would build the construct of "kitchenness."

Accommodation, on the other hand, represents an extended process of mapping new experience in light of past referents. Individuals search for a match between unknown phenomena and known schemata to explain their experiences in the world. When there is no solid match, the mind must radically modify or manipulate existing schemata through a kind of metaphoric system of reference, in order to interpret the unknown phenomena. Unlike analogy, in which an abstract pattern of relationships is produced, metaphor compares two separate domains for the purpose of achieving insight, to see *new connections.* I could describe my office to you more precisely than listing its properties if I explained that it is simply another clod fort. The walls are constructed of books, the door can be firmly locked, and I have been known to lob metaphorical "clods" over the walls of this fort and into the studio that lives near me. I also lob clods via the e-mail I emit from my little queendom. *Office as fort* is not a great stretch, but it helps you to make connections and understandings that are much deeper than simple description. This kind of accommodation allows the repertoire of schemata to grow and change over time.

The advantage of Piaget's interpretation of Kant's ideas of innate schemata is that it can account for changes over time. However, one difficulty with Piaget's model is that it does not explain the role of culture in the development of the individual. In response, Mark Gelernter, a noted scholar who studies the connections between architecture and different world views, suggests that, as individuals form their schemata, they do not do so alone; rather, they are guided through a combination of random experimentation, criticism, and encouragement. Directed by the behavior of individuals and society, and by the assumptions and world views of the culture, humans develop schemata that "fit" culturally within the world into which they are born.[7] Mental imagery and imagination are necessary components of assimilation and accommodation; as such, they play a significant and central role in this cognitive "construction" of the mind-world relationship. Memory, however, is modeled as a "storage" facility where a bank of images and knowledge are collected. It is an active facility, changing with time and influence, but its true potential, perhaps even its poetic potential, was not captured by Piaget.

A NEO-KANTIAN CONSTRUCTION

Susanne Langer, in *Philosophy in a New Key,* points out that the rise of Empiricism and its success in the physical sciences thrust the study of logic, metaphysics, aesthetics, and ethics aside, denying these ancient disciplines a place in modernity. "A passion for observation displaced the scholarly love of learned dispute, and quickly developed the experimental technique that kept humanity supplied thrice over with facts."[8] Empiricism replaced the mysteries as a belief system and created a method of inquiry meant to eradicate conjecture and replace it with a large measure of certitude. The crowning achievement of the Enlightenment, Empiricism enveloped Rationalism in its causes and creed. Every discipline wanted to be a "science," a status without which it was afforded no respect in the modern world. Psychology and sociology tried hard, but failed, to establish themselves as empirical sciences. The central principle of Empiricism always has been causation. For this reason, Empiricism has not been as fruitful for the human sciences as it has been for the physical sciences. In the human sciences of psychology and sociology, causation "does not engender leading questions or excite a constructive imagination. Instead of a method, it incites militant methodology."[9]

Karl Popper, in *The Logic of Scientific Discovery*, shook the empirical science community by challenging its claim that deductive reasoning had no place in inquiry.[10] At this point, the creed of induction slowly gave way to a recognition of how science was truly practiced. Langer's views about the place in science held by symbolic logic became more credible. Thus empirical science has moved away from its original intent and now points the way to what Langer refers to as a "New Key" for philosophy, the potential of Symbolism.

While Empiricism championed the establishment of a vast chasm between the inner and the outer worlds and extolled an objective technique of observation meant to avoid deductive reasoning, it curiously enough embraced one of the most "rational" and symbolic systems ever invented: mathematics. Throughout the rise of Empiricism, mathematics—a completely rational and symbolic, rather than factual, phenomenon—remained undisturbed. Early empirical inquiry involved direct observation through experimentation, as in Benjamin Franklin's study of electricity using a key and a kite. Yet, as empirical inquiry matured, its scientists became farther and farther removed from the actual phenomena of study and instead relied increasingly upon numerical machinations to symbolize relationships. Scientists watched needles, revolving drums, sensitive plates taking "readings," rather than directly or genuinely witnessing phenomena. They used concepts such as zero, infinity, square roots, negative numbers, imaginary numbers, infinite decimals, etc. These mathematical fantasies increasingly were tolerated by scientists until the basis of Empiricism—reliance upon observation of the world in order to induce "facts"—all but disappeared and, ironically, was

Significant Form

replaced with symbols. Science became less observation and more calculation. As Langer states, "Numbers and degrees and all their ilk only *mean* the real properties of real objects."[11] The result has been that science now works primarily with symbols, not phenomena, as the sense data: "The edifice of human knowledge stands before us, not as a vast collection of sense reports, but as a structure of facts that are symbols and laws that are their meanings."[12]

Langer defines two conceptions of Symbolism. One conception involves symbolic logic, the purpose of which is tracing general types and relations among abstracted forms, or concepts that lead to knowledge about things. Another conception involves psychiatry, emotion, religion, fantasy, and everything but knowledge; its purpose is in-sight. Both conceptions lead Langer to the conclusion that human *response* is a constructive, not a passive, phenomenon.

Langer's construction of the mind-body relationship can be classified as Neo-Kantian. Like Kant, Langer believes that the mind actively mediates between sensation and sense. She also asserts that the "forms" by which we construct the world are embodied in an inevitable link between symbol making and rationality, primary and basic capabilities of the human mind, neither of which is limited to linguistics alone. Kant limited his principles of form to the faculties of mind that were *constitutive,* rather than *interpretive,* of experience. Langer suggests that philosophical and scientific interest has shifted from an epistemological interest in the mind (how knowledge is sensed and acquired) to the realms of conception and expression. It is the introduction of Symbolic conception and expression that begins to tie the world of architectural designers to Langer's construction. The memorable image runs the gamut from conceptual to expressive. My memory of the California landscapes of my youth construct, in part, my understanding of the land and its use. Wholesale manipulation of water and land are parts of my "reality," and the human expression of power and control obviously is a part of my experience of dams, canals, and the political map of the San Joaquin Valley. These memorable images express all manner of human experience at different scales—personal, community, politics, global economy, and much more. These memories carry the symbols of humans striving to control and predict their future course.

The need to relate symbols to whatever they mean is a primary and ongoing function of the human mind. In Langer's words, symbol making is pre-rationative, but not pre-rational. It is fundamental to human thinking and is the basis of all ideation, being broader than thinking, fancying, or taking action. In Langer's construction, Symbolism has nothing to do with the iconographic functions that it normally is assigned in art; instead, symbols negotiate in-sight, not reference. A symbol is understood in the place where the idea it presents is conceived. My complex feelings of family history and relationships are symbolized in many ways by my grandmother's kitchen, with all its rich sensual delights and in all its social and communal dimensions. It is the conception, not the object, that a symbol directly *means*. My conception of "family" is triggered by various places in memory, one of which presents me with childhood's secretive sheltering of shared, communal places of the most intimate family variety. Langer concludes in *Feeling and Form* that symbol making is a rational act, because "any appreciation of form, any awareness of patterns in experience, is 'reason.'" It is a fundamental error to recognize rationality only in the phenomenon of systematic, explicit reasoning. "Rationality is the essence of mind, and symbolic transformation its elementary process."[13] Rationality is embodied in every mental act; moreover, rationality permeates the peripheral activities of the human nervous system, just as truly as it does the cortical functions.[14]

DISCURSIVE AND PRESENTATIONAL FORMS

In *Philosophy in a New Key*, Langer proposes two forms for human expression: discursive and presentational. Both discursive and presentational forms employ a logical structure for relating symbols to whatever they are to mean. In language, the logical structure of *discourse* unfolds in a linear (or hermeneutic) manner, encompassing the ability to relate words and their meaning to the concepts they symbolically represent. Language, as expression, is abstractly removed from experience and refers back to it. The *presentational* form of expression, on the other hand, is characterized by mental images which are expressions of memory. A mental image is a virtual object; its sensate character—images of visual form and space, movement, sound, touch, smell, and taste—is its entire being. For memorable experiences, the logical structure is holistic, encompassing the ability to relate an experience to the symbolic import it presents to consciousness. What emerges from memorable experience is the symbol of sentience (contact, retreat, participation, identity, love, grace, fear, sensuousness, intellect, intimacy, growth, expansiveness, reflection, communing, and more), of life in all its conflicts and meanings. These mental acts *present to* the mind the memory of the things, occasions, and parables of life.[15]

Because an unusual number of my memories include large, moving landscapes, it seems that I spent half my childhood in the back seat of a car, going somewhere. We generally lived in company housing on ranches in and around

Significant Form

the San Joaquin Valley in California. I always had a long bus ride to school, I rode in the back of the car when we went shopping or to the reservoirs for escape, and there were four or five trips across more than half of America, between Iowa (where our extended family was rooted) and California. All this I saw from the window of some vehicle—the one we seem to have had the longest, and of which my memory is most vivid, was a two-toned blue '47 Chevy two-door sedan, the back seat of which I shared with my brothers. (My one sister always complained of car-sickness if she rode in the back. I think she just did not want to endure my brothers; I was too young to make such demands.) It seemed perfectly natural to a child of California to live part of my life in a car and the other part moving from one ranch to another, as my father slowly improved his position. The car's window sill framed my view of the world. This rootlessness seems to be the source of my ability to move from place to place seeking my own career. While my education was interrupted repeatedly, what I received in return was my father's capacity to pick up and move wherever he pleased. My only anchor was my family, whose members either stayed in the San Joaquin Valley or spread out into other parts of the West to seek their own fortunes. So the memorable images I acquired from a car window seem to have propelled me into the life of a person who wanders, giving me the freedom to drift from place to place without fearing that I would not be able to anchor, even for a short time. The price of this form of freedom is a restlessness that does not always soothe the soul. But this freedom is who I am, in some very fundamental ways. The images from the car window allow me to dive into new situations, find my own level, and perform, even without many anchors.

The primary function of the mental image is to give us a cohesive conception—to form order from an originally disparate flux of sensations. The mental image and its active, imaginative reconstruction create order out of chaos, an order that is presentational in nature. Memorable imagery, unlike words, has no fixed meaning apart from the whole, no vocabulary that can be broken into basic units. Images, consciously or unconsciously, "fill the virtual space between us and reality."[16] Mental images are presented directly to our consciousness, where we may grasp, realize, comprehend, or ignore the import they contain. Their import is never fixed; rather, as these mental images are mixed with active conception, they may be manipulated through our imaginations to satisfy all kinds of present needs, inferring metaphoric connections and revealing significant meaning. Images have an ambivalence of content that words cannot have. They are wordless knowledge, not communication but in-sight. It is not the theme, accuracy, or fantasies of an image that stir us, but rather its ability to present human feeling, to present

68

life in its power, its sameness, its surprises, its sadness—its very existence. Whatever the effect, amazement and delight or isolation and fear, what is "known" is not discursive; what is expressed is direct, holistic, and presentational.

Mental images have a tendency to become metaphorical: they mean things. Metaphor has the power to change concepts as a result of its use in language. Even more, however, it is a *force* that makes life relational and intellectual, and creates new concepts. *Metaphor is the principle of the law of growth.*[17] By this, Langer means that we create new ideas, concepts, explanations, understandings, etc., by comparing past experience with a present situation. We are capable of imagining the relationship between two diverse experiences. We can imagine that a room meant for study should be like a tree house, if we have enough knowledge to support the comparison. If a designer approaches the unknown task in front of him or her—what should the place be "like?"—and imagines it as a tree house, certain characteristics and experiences are revealed that give the designer a feel for the nature of the place on the drawing board.

Mental imagery is used in ordinary life to help classify and categorize experience. Mental images are our readiest instruments for abstracting concepts, because they are the spontaneous embodiment of general ideas. They are the product of a rational mind, a mind searching for pattern and continually performing symbolic transformations. Using mental imagery metaphorically allows humans to find pattern in seemingly dissimilar referents. The potential to see one thing (an unknown design task) through a different lens (past place experience) is what allows design to happen, to grow, and to present new ideas for us to contemplate and integrate into memory.

The conceptual capacity to relate symbols to their meaning is the highest level of consciousness and rationality. It is the ability to name, to refer, and to intend in the absence of immediate stimuli. Whether this is done discursively through language and mathematics, or presentationally through imagination, it reflects the capacity to form relationships between things without their immediate presence. This capacity does not require a linkage to speech. The ability to form concepts developed well before speech and depends upon memory.[18] Memories are symbolic summations and elaborations of our unique experiences. They are essential to a healthy mind and are a central ingredient in creative thought. The utilitarian doctrine of symbols—that they satisfy biological needs—is simple-minded if it means that ritual, art, and dream cannot be construed under this model. Rather, the fundamental process of symbolization is claimed by Langer to be essential to thought;[19] without this process we could not define ourselves as the think-

Significant Form

69

ing, contemplating, action-oriented, and expressive beings that we are. The material of our experiences is "wrought" into symbolic meaning through a natural structural occurrence possible only in the processing of human minds. Again, as Edelman notes, this process evolved before language and, in fact, made the development of vocalization imperative for survival.

Because we apparently are "built" to conceptualize mentally through comparison and categorization, I asked the designers I interviewed to organize their own banks of images under thematic issues they felt were important to them and to name the categories they created. Also, because mental images are meaningful in many ways, I asked the designers to recategorize until they exhausted their repertoire of conceptualizations that they considered important. Each image, therefore, finds its way into more than one organization of themes. Although each individual image of place is unique, patterns of recurring domains emerged from this process: the secret place, the Arcadian place, the ancestral place, the shared place, the alone place, the intimate place, the gregarious place, places that stretch to meet the horizon line, and places that enclose and protect. Domains are symbolic of a quality and they are the structure of life. The significant form that they capture presents to us the essential nature of contact, retreat, participation, identity, love, grace, fear, sensuousness, intellect, intimacy, growth, expansiveness, reflection, sharing, communing, and more. Domains are symbolic because images of place present the vital and significant import of experience to our consciousness.[20]

It is true that memories are not particularly "accurate" in their depiction of past experience. Memories are never eidetic—that is, as detailed as a photograph. As time passes, our memory of original experience undergoes imaginative reconstruction.[21] However, the underlying significant form is not radically adjusted unless our psyches require it. Most architects and students involved in the memorable imagery study were convinced that the image, no matter how accurate, revealed its significant import even if details had faded. In fact, the community of people engaged in research seems to view these episodes of memorable experience as temporary "constructions" based on some immediate stimuli and not, as some have theorized, simply as past

experiences being stored in "long-term" memory.[22] If this is true, the theory of a fluid image bank is valid. Places seem to have significance in overlapping domains and may be remembered differently under different conditions. The designer's "use" of memory is free of any *one* construction. Instead, the construction is "manipulated and edited" for purposes that are entangled with the present design task.[23]

Existentialist phenomenologists believe that consciousness is embodied in the unselfconscious *actions* we take toward phenomena.[24] Symbolists believe that knowledge is embodied in a vast collection of mental constructions that are symbolic of logical and significant forms. These two world views pursue different ends: Existentialists pursue the foundations of human activity, while Symbolists (constructivists) pursue the foundations of knowledge. Existentialists do not presuppose one's existence as an object in the environment; rather, there is simply Being-in-the-World, with no distinction between mind, body, and world. Symbolists, for the most part, take up a constructive, interactive position—the world out there does exist, but we can only conceive of it within our own structures, building and evolving over time and experience.

Although Edelman is not a symbolist in any strict sense, he constructs a theory based on principles of neural evolution and selection. His theory presents a constructivist view of the relationship between self and world. The world impacts the mind/brain, but the mind has *a priori capacities* for selection and categorization, conceptualization, and symbolization.

A PRESENTATIONAL THEORY OF IMAGINATION

Our *imaginative* remembrance of things past creates our histories and actively shapes our present and future experience. The act of remembrance is not simply a collection of past perceptual experience or a nostalgic indulgence. Our ability to remember and to organize and reorganize past experience creates values, continually evolves to insure survival, and produces individual identity as well as human culture. The *remembered past* is *created* by interweaving perception, conception, memory, and imagination.

None of us can predetermine the meaning of our memories—our minds are opaque in the way they relate one experience to another. A touch, a taste, the smell of strawberries in the present, for instance, can shift past experience into focus. Meaning is constructed in the moment that memorable experience is merged with the present. It is a dance of correspondences, relationships, connections, associations, and linkages. The time of memory is not chronological—it is, in a way, iterative. Images of past experiences emerge, not as the experience originally existed, but changed, impacted, colored by all other experiences, by the present, and by possible futures.

Significant Form

Edelman suggests that there are many possible futures—that the future is not predetermined by the past, but is open and directed by human will. The suggestion here is that the past forms many potential avenues of action. Decisions about the nature of future places often are in the hands of architects and builders. One very important aspect that the research presented here did not address is the manner in which important habitual gestures and paths may be embedded in memorable place. However, most architects and student designers remembered what can only be termed archetypal images. They tended to be places that originated in youth (tree houses, forts, secret gardens), places they have since reinvented over and over again in their design careers. These images are not always "practical" or causal, but they are expressive of human living. Architecture is one of many expressive acts. It is a development of communication about places and the settings of being human.

Furthermore, while it is true that people do not have identical impressions, their respective concepts of things, events, or others embody the same or similar concepts.[25] We can say this is true because we deduce it from our ability to understand one another. We would still be living in caves, if we existed at all, if we didn't have a universal capability for symbolization, conceptualization, communication, and—most important to this discussion—imagination. Through memorable imagery, we see meaning abstractly, rebuild conceptions and symbolizations from past experience, and propose future conceptualizations by passing meaning from one context to another.

Chapter 4

Communicating Meaning

SUSANNE LANGER STATES, in *Introduction to Symbolic Logic*, that we have two kinds of knowledge: knowledge *of* things and knowledge *about* things. Knowledge *of* a thing is directly sensual: the feel, taste, smell, sound, movement, or look of a thing in the phenomenal world. Knowledge *about* a thing, in contrast, requires conceptualization—a more abstract way of being in the world. Knowledge *about* a thing includes its relationship to context, how it is made up, and how it functions. To have knowledge *about* a thing, it is necessary to know the *logical form* it possesses beyond its sensual characteristics. I may know *of* a plaza—its smell, texture, how one moves through it, how sounds reverberate within it. If I want to know *about* this same plaza—how it is organized; how it relates to political and cultural identity; how it is enclosed by façades that are complex and have changed through time; how it is used by the people who work, live, and visit there; and how it is similar to, and different from, other plazas that I have experienced—then I have knowledge that involves meaning, interpretation, and abstraction. To know *about* something, I have discovered that it has "logical form."

The discovery of logical form in seemingly disparate phenomena requires the human capacity for *analogous thinking*. According to Langer, analogous thinking is a natural, logical intuition. She states, "The great value of analogy is that by it, and it alone, we are led to seeing a single 'logical form' in things which may be entirely discrepant as to content."[1] For example, after identifying the logical form of the central axis, one can identify it in both a cathedral and a house. One can use a rhythm from a particular dance to design an elaborate stair or path. One can understand the degree of enclosure that defines a plaza as similar to the enclosure of a southwestern courtyard house. Analogies require a logical relationship between referents—

between house and cathedral, rhythm and stair, plaza and courtyard. Knowledge *about* the world is gained through this "natural intuition," as Langer calls it. By any other definition, this ability to think analogously, and therefore to categorize, would be considered "innate" to the human mind.

CATEGORIZATION AND ANALOGOUS THINKING

The sort of language designers used in response to my questions about memorable places indicated what I would term a growing maturity of expression and assurance. The expressions which freshmen and sophomores used to refer to a rich set of images were rather limited—one word or simple phrases expressed the content of the categorizations they named. Graduate students used more complex language. Sometimes their responses were poetic. Professionals, on the other hand, had difficulty expressing the meaning of their categories with simple phrases. Often their descriptions of what was important were complex and expressed multiple concerns. The professionals, while sharing similar conceptualizations of place with the students, expressed themselves in language that often passed beyond the poetic to profound observations about themselves, society, culture, and humanity, as seen through the places in their memories. This in no way infers that the student groups *thought* less meaningfully about their experiences, only that they either had not yet gained an expressive language or had not developed the assurance to use it in their presentation of ideas.

The ability to categorize through analogous thinking is described by most of the authorities referenced in this book. Many conclude the same thing: we categorize our experiences by grouping "like" things. If something we encounter is "unlike" the things we have experienced before, we tend to try to find a similar "logical form" that will allow us to conceptualize this particular experience. There is some disagreement about whether the word *analogy* or the word *metaphor* should be used to describe the workings of our minds. Both terms are relevant. Earl MacCormac offers the most satisfying distinction I have found. He suggests that analogy and metaphor are simply ends of a continuum. In producing an analogy, one compares referents that are more "similar" than dissimilar. At the other end of the continuum is metaphor, where one compares referents that are more "dissimilar" than "similar." At one end of the spectrum, one can compare one plaza with another plaza that has quite similar characteristics. At the other end of the spectrum, one could compare a particular plaza to a circus or a dance—dissimilar referents that may share some logical form.[2]

As designers sorted the cards on which I had recorded each memorable place they had named, they were inventing themes, such as quality of light, and then dividing each category into variations on that theme, such as: these places are dark and shadowy, the light in these places varies across the day, the light in these places is strong and direct, the light in these places is soft and glowing. They put an image like Grandmother's kitchen into the same category with one like Frank Lloyd Wright's Fallingwater, because they felt that the two shared something—a logical form that knit these places together as having "similar" light. This ability to categorize seemingly different experiences defines each category as loosely aligned through a formal logic of place. In the next sort, the designer might well recategorize these two images and cast them into different categories under a different theme, suggesting that, under this sorting, there is no logical form that is shared between these particular referents.

LANGUAGE AND METAPHOR

As I reviewed the language with which designers described the thematic and categorical concepts they discovered as they sorted their past experiences of place, it was clear that the language used contained embodied metaphors. During my original research, I was not studying the design process directly, so I did not collect drawings or record design sessions. What I had were the expressions people used to explain in their own words meaningful categories and themes they had developed. These are what I had recorded. Lakoff and Johnson, in *Metaphors We Live By*,[3] suggest that there are different kinds of *embodied* metaphorical references, the most common of which are *orientational* metaphors and *conduit* metaphors. Orientation and conduit are the resulting logical forms that can be shared between seemingly different referents. Conceptual embodiment refers to the fact that we think about the world in terms of our bodies' relationship to the environment. Thus, we appropriate words to describe the location or movement of our bodies through the environment and then express abstract concepts metaphorically. We say, for example, that time progresses, although time in itself shows no physical movement. Or we may say that truth emerges, although truth has no physical surroundings from which to emerge. These concepts, then, are "embodied," in the sense that we speak of them as if they, in fact, have physical bodies. This way of thinking about abstract concepts is the fundamental way in which we understand the world. It predates speech; indeed, speech itself is based upon our embodied state.

The designers whom I interviewed used metaphoric references to explain the content of their places and themes. Embodied metaphors permeate

Communicating Meaning

the language we all use to locate ourselves in the world and communicate the meaning of our experiences. Lakoff and Johnson describe the human ability to address modal shifts in the act of referencing. *Modal shifts* are those that require abstract conceptual ideas to be expressed through sensate analogy. If I describe a house from my youth as foreboding, I am shifting my concept of the house, a physical object, by adding a human psychological presence to it; thus I am applying one mode to another.

For Lakoff and Johnson, the use of embodied metaphors is *experientially based*. According to them, thought and action provide the first framework for our construction of the world. Later, we use embodied metaphors in language as a way of expressing our physical anchors to our *bodies-in-the-world*. Conceptualization is both created and refined by embodied metaphors, so much so that embodied metaphors play a central role in our mental life. Put simply, metaphors are central to our expression of meaning and are translated from embodiment—our experiences in the world—into language. Metaphors as linguistic expressions are possible precisely because they make up our conceptual system, and are based upon embodied experience. Metaphor is, therefore, not only thought but also action. The comparisons we make between referents in our ceaseless categorizations are *real,* not simply a result of language. The terms we use in everyday language reveal the critical importance of the body and its extension into space, its sensing of the world.

ORIENTATION METAPHORS OF PLACE

Metaphors that *orient* are those that use spatial orientation to convey meaning. Embodied orientation requires a reference to the body-in-the-world, and orientational metaphors rely on this em-body-ment for their meaning. In my research, for example, several designers sorted their image banks according to whether they wanted to return to, or not to return to, a particular place. This returning is a body-oriented metaphor used to explain an emotional response, a connection with the past where there may be a choice to revisit. In its most literal sense, a return is to turn back, a *turning of the body* to face back to contemplate an earlier time and place. Designers who named this theme were sympathetic, perhaps, to the notion of feeling embodied in Thomas Wolfe's famous dictum, *You Can't Go Home Again.* In appendix 2, Karen Cordes Spence mentions the distortion of memorable images from youth, as she describes a return to the backyard of her youth: "It was equally amusing to visit the deep, dark forest with its gigantic rock formations in my childhood backyard and to find only a few large shade trees with rocks that might measure four feet in diameter." The designers who identified *returning* as a significant aspect of memorable places were referring to a desire for physical reconnection to a memorable place or, conversely, a desire to return to the experience in memory only, with no need to return physically and, perhaps, disturb an originally meaningful memory.

Patterns played a role in orienting designers as well. They spoke of places having a musical pattern, historical pattern, geometrical pattern, numerical pattern, or typological pattern, or exhibiting a datum of some sort. This is orientation by configuration or gestalt. The term *gestalt* here is taken in an experiential sense, to mean "the whole that we humans experience as more basic than the parts."[4] Some statements further implied orientation by reference to connection, affixing, or binding, as in statements—both experiential and emotional—concerning the formation of an "attachment" to a place. Designers also spoke frequently of being "connected" to the outer world of sea, land, and universe, or spoke of the opposite, of being connected to someplace "inside."

Lifetime orientations were elaborated through metaphors of having "sides" of life; that is, tranquil or busy. "My life in progression" is a theme that indicates an orientation of constant forward movement—life being seen as a series of *advances* or as a *continuity* of development. Many other body-in-the-world terminologies were used frequently. Such common terms as *exposure,* to un*cover* or dis*cover,* as well as the act of being *in-between,* betwixt, among, or amid—all these suggest an orientation to be *in* a minor space or place that separates two or more major, committed, or named places, events, or occasions. To *encounter,* impact, meet, approach, or confront means to meet head on, at times physically and at other times symbolically or imaginatively. To be *grounded* often was used to suggest feeling supported, stuck, fixed, or transfixed bodily, experientially, or emotionally. Being *located* in space—placed or positioned physically—is one of the most common body metaphors that orient designers in memory.

Other body metaphors involve relating one place to another and can be thought of as either orientation metaphors or, in some cases, conduit metaphors that relate one kind of thing to another, different kind of thing. To be *in relation to* a place, activity, or person could be to compare, connect, or involve an individual with place as if they were the same entities. *Interlocking* or *linking* events, people, or places can mean interconnection or interrelation in some mad circle.

Other expressions that suggest embodiment are the *sides* of an issue, the *stages* of something, the *sides of my life,* or places that *stand* to either right or left, or before or after. The *stages of self-emergence and independence* suggest a symbolic embodiment orienting issues that are emotional. *How places impressed me* was a common phrase, as if the place stampeded over the speakers, marking them indelibly and unforgettably. Speaking of the *interactions* between built forms suggests that buildings have dialogues or some kind of social life—another example of orientation via our body-in-the-world experience.

MEASURE AS A METAPHOR FOR PLACES

Designers often used notions of *degrees* and *levels* to indicate the amount of some quality. Phrases like *degrees of how well known* places were, or the *levels of complexity,* employed orientational metaphors to indicate a kind of measuring that, while not physical, was experiential. These are common terms—usually such opposing measures as high/low, strong/weak, major/minor, positive/negative, large/small, significant/insignificant—that clarified what the designer meant, indicating that a meaning could not be conveyed as readily without the metaphorical reference to measurement. These measurements were related to emotionally charged, experientially felt, or objectively abstracted references to place.

METAPHORS OF PLACE THAT CONTAIN AND PERSONIFY

Container metaphors are those that model referents as being *inside* something or somewhere. Designers often referred to the act of being *enclosed* by space, using such notions as close around, circumscribe, surround, internalize. Such concepts stands in contrast to the vast, open, or *exposed* space of some architecture and landscapes. *Protected spaces*—those that are *guarded* in some manner—speak of the body as being defended on all sides or as positioned with its *back* against a wall, as the *front* watches. *Confined spaces* speak of containers that are tightly bounded—limited, narrow, or constrained. Spaces that are *surrounded* orient designers through boundaries that can be identified by the body's senses; these either besieged or circumscribed the designer. *Inclusive spaces* contain by including, comprising, or involving, and often reveal a social response to "others."

Container metaphors that *personify* place are among those occurring most commonly in designers' language. These references to spaces ascribe human qualities or feelings to places. Designers frequently described places as intimate, bustling, inspired, dictated, generated, controlled, friendly, restrained, reactionary, articulate, creative, charged, arrested, inundated, liberated, dominated, powerful, influential, possessive, speaking, whimsical, delightful, romantic, spiritual, severe, comfortable, poetic, mysterious, fast, moody, giving, dynamic, protected, orderly, sophisticated, significant, sensate, humanistic,

Remembrance and the Design of Place

impassioned, intellectual, evocative, involved, emotional, communicative, secure, fearful, dependent, obligatory, affective, impressive, threatening, stimulating, felt. Designers, like all humans, infuse places with human characteristics in order to convey meaning and purpose.

EVALUATIVE METAPHORS OF PLACE

Cultural coherence metaphors reflect fundamental values that are apparent in the designers' statements. Designers referred to architecture as *high* or *low,* or as *formal* or *informal* in nature. These body metaphors are culturally attuned to good/bad and known/unknown value systems. The metaphors themselves indicate a value comparison. *Levels* of importance indicate another culturally driven, value-laden hierarchy that has meaning in terms of a social contract. Even actions, such as getting *high* on certain architecture ("feeling" good), are culturally profound body metaphors. Most of these value referents are oriented to the body and could be understood cross-culturally. Although orientations might vary ("high" in another culture might have a negative connotation), the fact remains that all humans, the societies they form, and the cultures to which those societies belong, use value-laden body/action metaphors to understand and communicate ideas.

PLACES AS METAPHORS

Conduit metaphors, while a bit more subtle, are used lavishly by designers. Structuring one concept in relation to another is quite common. The metaphor of an *illuminating place* is an example of phraseology that allowed a designer to describe a place as personally meaningful rather than as well lit. The *strength of a memory* is also a way of indicating the ability to recall easily, and the power of the recollection. Conduit metaphors abounded, as different modes of place, people, or activities were juxtaposed. *Light as drama, a context of ideas, the strength of context, the geometry of light, a higher self* to be found in certain places—all these relate the use of body metaphors to *enlighten* meaning, to help the designer understand and communicate the significance of memorable past place experience. Other examples include *integration as patchwork, the shape of darkness, place as refuge, place as solace, experience as a series of fragments, place as a stage sets, landscape in the mind, place as color,* and *the transmission of quiet.*

In appendix 14, Thomas Sofranko gives us an example of a metaphor in design used to convey an idea about a place: "*Iscariotic Bistro* is a risk-taker's place of repast. The straight and narrow path leads to a precarious landing.

fig. 21. Iscariotic Bistro, by Thomas Sofranko

There profound detachment serves as a gentle reminder of the need for separation and introspection, while simultaneously antagonizing the paranoid neuroses of every patron. *Iscariotic Bistro,* the perfect place for a zealous zealot's ego to enjoy a last supper." Sofranko goes on to describe how the designer finds substance in memory and the struggle to make an abstract idea, intentions, and emotions visible. Metaphors help to frame an abstract idea long enough to examine its potential for a future place.

MEMORY AS DYNAMIC COMMUNICATION

Our memories are more dynamic than simple analogous categorizations. At a very simple level, memory is the ability to repeat a performance. In memory, however, repetition, in the true sense of the word, is impossible. The mind, unlike a computer (whose ability to repeat *exactly* often has been used as an analogy for thought), does not remember places, people, events, and experiences eidetically. If strict repetition were the mind's primary ability, human evolution would have been impossible. Instead, we learn to categorize experience and in turn revise those categories as time and new experiences dictate. The mind is a vigorously processing, biological entity which categorizes and recategorizes incoming experience, mixes it with existing knowledge and import, and creates concepts and symbols that form and influence our thoughts, feelings, experiences, and interactions with others. Human survival depends on this ability to adapt and evolve through the fluid ordering of experience and knowledge. Accordingly, each memorable place image changes and adjusts to fit our needs and desires.[5]

Our image banks are established through particular, original experiences of places and events which are colored by our individual physical, psychological, social, and cultural filters. Each memorable place image that we recall has content—that is, it holds, in addition to the present act of remembrance, our impressions of the physical characteristics of the particular place, the way people behave in it, the qualities of its milieu, and our emotional responses to it. If we understood each experience we encountered as a completely new and isolated occurrence, we would not display the categorical and symbolic behavior that is so distinctively human. Without some ordering of experience, we would be unable to stay sane or communicate with each other. Consequently, life and language abound with metaphor—the ordering of experience according to embodiment. Designers, in turn, use the understanding of the world provided by the interlacing of embodiment and personal memorable experience to transfer meaning from the past to the future.

As was noted earlier, analogic thinking and metaphoric thinking are pro-

Communicating Meaning

81

cesses all humans use to understand circumstance and express meaning. Architects, like artists in other disciplines, may use these processes more liberally to convert physical, bodily understandings into meaningful referents which are both complex and abstract. Lakoff and Johnson suggest that the identification of *gestalts* is the key manner by which humans "categorize" objects, not in a classical item-listing way, "but in terms of prototypes and family resemblances."[6] They consider "causation" a model that we employ in everyday life. If an action, orientation, or identification occurs over and over, these occurrences are "loosely" categorized; that is, we experience them as a *gestalt,* wherein the whole (category) is more basic than the parts. These categories are "loose," in the sense that, while basic and holistic, they are also "indefinitely analyzable."[7] This allows the designer to construct and reconstruct memorable experience in a way that allows each reconstruction to reveal different facets of the experience, depending on the needs of present circumstance or the designers' imagined future.

One analogy or metaphor usually is insufficient to describe our full experience of a place. As the designers in this study sorted and then resorted their banks of images, they applied different analogies and metaphors to explain the meanings these places held for them. This categorization and recategorization speaks to the dynamic nature of memory. The ability to "see" more than one particular meaning for any one particular place image is the secret of the fullness of remembered experience. Designers "see" many facets of meaning for any one place image. The studied "use" of memorable experience therefore can be selective and precise, in contrast to the messy and multi-valent "whole" original experience.

PRIMARY AND HIGHER-ORDER CONSCIOUSNESS

Humans exist on several levels at once. Primary consciousness, according to Edelman, is the kind of consciousness we share with other animals. It is a basic "mapping" of experience in the brain that correlates scenes and produces biological values for certain repeated, necessary conditions—food, shelter, procreation, sense of community, sense of position and place, and so on. This type of consciousness is limited to the remembered present.[8] A higher-order consciousness is available only to beings who create symbolic reference, evolve semantic capabilities, and develop language. Categorization is the primary capability of the human mind that relates our bodies to a personal history through internal criteria and constraints.[9] For survival purposes, the mind learns from value-driven categorization. It then develops a socially constructed self that is aware of itself, has the ability to name things and ideas, has intentions towards things and ideas, and refers between past and future.

The explosion of self-consciousness sets the stage for the physical and emotional desire for communication. This flowering of past primary consciousness into a higher order of awareness required a new kind of memory, one in which "the conceptual centers of the brain treat the symbols and their references and the imagery they evoke as an 'independent' world to be further categorized."[10] Edelman's description of higher-order consciousness, based on the biological research underpinning his theories of Neural Darwinism, is very close to Langer's proposal of the mental image as a "virtual" object.[11] Both believe that we can contemplate the meanings of mental images and categorize them according to "scenes" and "memories," i.e., the constructed mental objects provided by consciousness. Global mappings—the physical "strengthening" of connections by way of categorizations and recategorizations of experience—are dynamic, necessarily involving our bodies and our personal histories.[12] The dynamics are driven by qualitative values, shifting as experience adds to memory and challenges established personal and social meanings.

ANALOGY, METAPHOR, AND DESIGN

Metaphor—the mapping of one thing onto another in a different domain—is apparent in our discursive form of reasoning. Its basis, however, lies in our worldly actions and internal orderings. According to Lakoff and Johnson, the language we create is an extension of our bodily existence in the world. Metaphor is thought and action. The ceaseless categorizations that arise as a result of our comparisons are *real* and not simply a result of language; they result in concepts and thoughts that are basically metaphorical. Analogic thinking and metaphoric thinking are the catalysts, and form the framework, for the human ability to understand. As a result, they also are significant for the act of design. Analogy and metaphor help us to order the unknown in reference to the known, the part in reference to the whole, and past meaningful experience for use in present and future situations.[13]

Because analogy and metaphor are basically *acts* of understanding, these embodied acts are also basic to design. Design is a practice. Design is an *act* of understanding and the pragmatic *use* of past experience to identify, peruse, and imagine possible futures. It is important that designers realize their dependency upon past experience and approach this process critically. A critical analysis could consist of a hermeneutic "dipping" into the past—a communication that leads to understanding. It must then, however, be turned to some pragmatic use if meaning is to evolve and illuminate human life in places.

Communicating
Meaning

Chapter 5

Intentional Frameworks
in the Act of Design

[Place] has colour, depth, density, and
solidity, it has associations and symbols, it
both offers possibilities for and yet restricts
experience. Thus a prairie is "vast," a
mountain "impassable," a house "spacious,"
or a street "constricted" only with reference
to a particular human intention.

—E. Ralph, *Studies in Classic American Literature*

ONVERSING IN IMAGERY is a common occurrence when designers are working. Informal conversations among designers often include references to memorable places described and discussed for a multitude of reasons. At work, these conversations in imagery often are directed toward both the memorable past place experience and its implications for a design task at hand. Samples of dialogue by practicing architects may illustrate designers' intentional use of memorable images. Littlejohn's record of conversation between two architects, Charles Moore and William Turnbull, working on aspects of the 1984 Louisiana World Exposition, exemplifies the way architects converse in imagery.

"I was wondering," Bill Turnbull suggests, as he lays in more pencil lines on the uppermost of a dozen drawings, "if maybe you wanted to do something like that Florentine thing, when the two passageways split?"
"What Florentine thing?"

"You know. Where you come out past the David statue, and that gallery splits going down to the river."

"The Uffizi?"

"Yeah. Because that would give you the space on the axis, and the beginning of the Empress's walk as something very special on the inside."

Moore adds some more lines to the sketch. "Is this what you mean?"

"Something like that, and then the back does . . . whatever the back does. We could just use the wall of whatever White Elephant was next to it." Turnbull draws some more.

"That's quite amusing," Moore concedes. "Now *this* could be solid." Everyone is now either drawing or watching others draw.

"And this would be what you'd do with the steps."

"You know," Charles says, after a significant pause. "I think we've hit on one of the eternal verities."

From that moment on, this cleverly splayed intersection, which connects Charles' trash-compacted Piranesi Wonderwall with Dmitri Vedensky's dowager empress's promenade, is locked into the design. Charles refers to it as "Bill's Uffizoik effusion."[1]

This conversation in imagery illustrates the architects' intention to use a memorable place in a certain way. In this particular case, these designers intend an *experiential* passage in a memorable place (a path through the Uffizi) to transfer to a future place. They move forward by objectifying the rhythm, meter, body movement, and attributes of the original place and suggesting them as a possible solution to the task at hand. Their "intention" toward the remembered place is translated here as experiential (extending the sensuous body), with concomitant physical ramifications.

The path of the Uffizi presents a complex image. In this case, a designer's memory was triggered by the task facing him; pursuit of a solution suggested a past experience. The memorable image of the Uffizi path was used to order the unknown future place through the experience of movement. The designers' involvement with "the path of the Uffizi" at the time of this design project would not preclude the possibility of using the memory of "the path of the Uffizi"—or, indeed, some other aspect of the experience (touch, taste, smell, light, color, volume, etc.)—in some other context to solve a different problem. In other words, the same image can be intended experientially, emotionally, or objectively to guide the response to potential place making in any project if the designer sees it as applicable. An image can be assigned different intentions, depending on the designer's attitude or objective.

Intentional Frameworks

fig. 22. Negotiation,
by Mark Lochrin

*Remembrance
and the
Design of Place*

Intentionality may play an important role in understanding the range of concerns any one image may present to the same individual at different times and under different circumstances. At one point, a designer may remember a hometown or backyard tree house as a fond memory with personal implications; at other times, that same image may be appropriated for its sensuous qualities, communal capacities, emotional charge, or attributes of organization and order when applied to design. Intentionality may account for the complexity of remembrance in individuals across time and across circumstances.

86

Mark Lochrin's game of Spatial Solitaire is suggestive of this overlap of meaning and intention. He draws a series of backyards woven into an adventure for Bugs Bunny, the trickster. The objective of the memory is to understand the issue of negotiation. At the time when Lochrin played this game, negotiation was the theme that captured his memory of backyard play—a "field" that was ripe for all kinds of occurrences. Lochrin's intention toward his design was to capture this quality, perhaps running through emotion, experience, and intellectual content in various phases of thought: "The place stemmed from a memory of a series of backyards, adjacent to or near the house where I grew up. Also included are fences and front gates. The 'stiles' represent openings in the fences or fences frequently scaled. Memorable trees, or trees that served as tree houses, are also noted. There is a sort of black screen, but I don't know what this stands for. . . . The representation is more of a two-dimensional key to the literal location of significant memories within an actual territory of childhood play, as well as the suggestion that these locations possibly are doors to other trains of memory" (appendix 15).

The mind has no static constructions; it continually reconstructs organized categories in order to fit new, incoming experience. Some constructions are more stable than others, but all are subject to retrofit in responding, adjusting, or constructing complex world experiences. But memorable places do not often come and go in our minds without some stimulus that triggers the reinterpretation of a particular place experience or abstractions drawn from these experiences. Generally, places are complex enough to be remembered for different purposes, depending upon circumstances in the present. Remembered places change import like chameleons, according to need, situation, or purpose. In one instance, a tree house—a common and powerful place experience for American designers—could be recalled from memory for the purpose of examining such components of experiential significance as climbing above the ground plane, the feel of planed wood against natural wood, dappled light, the sound of wind and rustling leaves—for its experiential, sensuous content. Or, the tree house could be recalled for the purpose of examining such components of emotional significance as a sense of removal to a secret place, a feeling of control, or a time of sharing with special friends. Yet again, the tree house can present the designer with more abstracted ideas of organization—the potential of multiple levels; the power of a small, fragile structure being supported by a much more powerful one— or perspectival shifts from small to large, up to down, and inside to outside.

Intentional Frameworks

Each memorable place has this same elasticity; each can be stretched to meet any purpose the designer feels is relevant to a current task, and each can be mined for its complex, interwoven, and suggestive characteristics. "I have absolutely no idea," says Steven Moore, "why I connected Martin Heidegger to a bicycle that I have not recalled for thirty-three years. Such speculation is, without the skills of Jungian analysis, not a very productive enterprise. It seems enough to appreciate the possible mysteries that the relation might illuminate—both about Heidegger as a referent and about myself as a designer" (appendix 16).

The term *intention* has a history of meaning in both common and philosophical uses. The root of the term, *intension,* comes from Latin and means "to stretch out." Commonly, the word is used to signify "be attentive to" something. Philosophically, *intention* has a more complex history. The first significant use important for this essay was by Franz Brentano, who, in his desire to create a descriptive psychology, concluded that his new classification of psychic phenomena would be characterized by reference to contextual directedness to an object. Whatever is before the mind, he said, will be a representation, a judgment, or a phenomenon of love or hate. In all cases, there is an object (concrete or abstract, real or imagined) to which the mental act is directed.[2]

Edmund Husserl continued the use of the term *intentionality* in his development of phenomenology. Under Husserl, phenomenology emerges as a science "concerned with mental images being capable of extracting essence from experience or fantasy."[3] Husserl was most concerned with the subjective processes of humans and their potential for isolating the irreducible essences of the phenomena of our intentions—the things we intend to do.

> Design is the death of memory. The design idea, formulated from memory fragments, is a temporary construct often lacking the fortitude or clarity necessary for the designer to use it as an intelligible communicative device. Occasionally, however, an idea emerges between fragments with such precision and clarity that the conscious mind can extract it from the subconscious and the designer can make the memory concrete. In the design process, as ideas become tangible, the memory loses its translucent, transitory, multidimensional complexity—in effect, the memory dies and is replaced by a physical marker (the constructed architecture). This marker, much like a tombstone, remains as the residue of what once was. (Thomas Sofranko, appendix 14)

These phenomena related to our intentions pervade our awareness. Husserl believed that, in our streams of consciousness, we are aware of a distinction between processes of intending and objects as intended. "Since all meaning is intentional and meaning is constituent to consciousness," he argued, "both sides of this distinction are intentional. That is to say, we are not referring here to objects as things in an outer world, but things intended."[4] The phenomenological attitude that Husserl presents in his work perpetuates the subject/object dichotomy and proposes that there *is* a world out there; but it is a world mediated not by innate structures of the mind, as Kant proposed, but by our intentions toward the object, real or imagined. For Husserl, the world can never be known concretely, but we can come to know its essence through the structured "bracketing" of our experience. This bracketing is thought to sort out the subconscious philosophical, psychological, and experiential aspects of the world; at the end of this process, we may comprehend our own intentions. Husserl's intentionality provides a structure that an individual can "consult" and suggests what can be "known" if it is targeted.[5]

In the material from the design interviews conducted for this study, I find many ways in which designers "consult" their image banks of memorable places while searching for clues to an approach for a design project. However, it is unclear how much of this process or its results are "known" by the designer who is targeting past place experience. An important implication of this view is that the emphasis in intentionality is toward acts, or human practices, not the physical object itself. I suggest that, in many ways, this process of consulting and targeting, carried out by the designer through intentional states, is as often a subconscious action as it is a conscious action. This begs the question as to whether architects would be better designers if they were more aware or better trained in intentionally accessing useful mental imagery.

Traditional masonry buildings are reinterpreted using earth-colored concrete block and mortar—an industrialized masonry assembly which responds to the technology of the present. The scale of the blocks records the effort of the individual craftsperson in their assembly. The metal roof which floats above the building simultaneously differentiates the walls as belonging to the earth and the roof as belonging to the sky, reduces the heat gain on the building, and helps move air between the two roofs. Saltillo floors and Arizona sandstone act as thermal maps and recall the building traditions of northern Mexico and the Southwest. The residence mimics the color of the landscape of the site and mountains beyond the exterior, while the interior is brightly colored and recalls urban vernacular architecture in Mexico. (Ed Burian, appendix 10)

Intentional
Frameworks

There is a significant difference between the way Husserl approached intentionality and the way existentialists like Heidegger defined the term. Husserl always referred to an exterior world to which consciousness was directed.

This subject/object distinction then could allow different individuals to form different constructions of meaning, and "none of these meanings would coincide with the object."[6] Meanings, then, are constructed through the activity of the mind and are not revealed by probing the object itself. So, each time architects consult their own memorable place imagery, they may be "reconstructing" their own relationships to it differently than they had in earlier constructions or would in future constructions. If this is so, each time we access a memorable place image, our intentions toward it allow the place to be reconstructed within a different framework. I can only conclude that this framework would be contextual, involving the particular setting, people, and politics; a particular time of life; seasons; outside forces; the significance of a present situation in which the designer is functioning; and the growing maturity of the designer. Any of these could alter intentions from one remembered instance of place to the next time it is called upon for assistance.

In Heidegger's use of intentionality, he tries to avoid the subject/object dialectic and replaces it instead with an "involved, meaning-giving, *doing* subject."[7] Heidegger is trying to avoid the notion of mental content as primary and suggests that one has no self-referential experience of oneself as causing an activity. Instead, Heidegger sees the individual as "coping" with day-to-day existence through the experience of acting in the world—the steady flow of skillful activity in response to one's sense of the environment. This view of intentionality suggests that the designer, in "coping" with the project at hand, does not separate a memorable place image from *using* it in the act of design. The designer, the mental image, and the expression on paper all are one continuous flow of action in a coping mode. Dreyfus perceives Heidegger to mean:

> a small part [of our immediate coping] is spent in the deliberate, purposeful, subject/object mode, which is, of course, the mode we tend to notice, and which has therefore formed our common-sense concepts and been studied in detail by philosophers.
>
> [In contrast,] skillful coping does not require a mental representation of its goal at all. It can be *purposeful* without the agent entertaining a purpose.[8]

By this, Dreyfus means that "it is not the *mind* which is thinking about something, but the *embodied person* going about his or her business." The purpose of utilizing imagery during the design process is embodied in the act—it is there implicitly rather than explicitly. The designer is simply "being" a designer—coping with the world of designing future places by remembering past place experience that is applicable in some way. Dreyfus, however, does distinguish between the beginning doer and the expert doer. In our case, the beginning designer is probably working out a design through slow and deliberate acts that are somewhat self-conscious. The expert designer simply "works" the act of design because he or she has "practiced" the rule-bound behavior over a span of time—it is this doing/acting individual who perhaps is less conscious of her or his own processes. The use of past place experience in design is almost pure reaction, pure "coping" in action. It is probably only when they must explain themselves to others—builders, clients, users—that designers become more aware of how they reach certain conclusions in design.

> The first level of subjective memory—the frames that I recall in the process of design—is alternately filled by images, smells, sounds, or touches that seemingly are evoked by the conditions of a site itself. These resonances between the present and the past are phenomenological in nature—meaning that they cannot be explained in objective terms, only experienced and appreciated as a subjective form of knowledge. These memories are not quantifiable measures to which we have willful access, but are seemingly random connections to the categories of private experience that normally are concealed from consciousness. . . .
>
> Sites also recall figures—the second level of memory that I experience in the process of design. By *figures,* I mean the *a priori* forms and networks implicit in the local conditions of the place itself. As soon as I lay an axis across representation of the site (say, from one hilltop to another), or draft the angles of the summer and winter sun, or place the project in an economic context, memory is triggered. This formal memory is not of personal history, nor of learned antecedents, but of Kantian categories—circles and squares, public and private, and so forth. The struggle for me as a designer—and, I suspect, for us all—is to *remember* the figures implicit in the site itself, to bring forth the *multiple* figures that are possible there, rather than to impose a single abstract order upon the site that is unrelated to what exists on the ground. In this sense, exploring a place through design is an act of cultural remembering. The structures of space and of society must be made present in our act of design. (Steven Moore, appendix 16)

Intentional Frameworks

The act of design seems to be an intentional "coping" with the unknown by referencing the known. Intentionality is a structure that we can "consult" only when we put it out of the immediacy of the act and consider it from some distance. This is what designers did with their memorable place images as they constructed themes and categories. They had the ability to transcend their own experiences, to use them to imagine other people and places, to discover something new and surprising, and to deepen a thought. This describes the powerful intentionality that a designer displays toward the rich potential of the role which remembrance can play in the act of making places. The elasticity of a designer's mind, his or her capacity to adjust a place image to many different circumstances, is a prerequisite for the ability to "imagine" in design, to retrieve an idea with the intention to use it in a certain way.

Husserl suggests that the history of the ideas that are tied up in an "act" of intentionality can be targeted, understood, dissected, and contemplated. Designers, however, usually do not concern themselves as much with the structure of the act itself as they do with its purpose, which is to convey meaning first to themselves and then, through the use of memorable experiences and places, to the design task at hand. In this sense, the view of intentionality as purposeful activity is a pragmatic one, wherein the designer, while working on a project, refers to past place experience and displays intentionality toward the design project.

The "directedness" of the designer's intentionality has three paths: emotional, experiential, and objective. Each memorable image of place can present several domains symbolic of the "life" lived or imagined in those places. However, designers also display a fluidity across intentionality—the difficult mixture of meaning, purpose, and human will, through which are expressed contact, retreat, participation, identity, love, grace, sensuousness, intellect, intimacy, growth, expansiveness, reflection, communing, and more. As the participants in my research created titles for the memorable places they sorted, and names for categories, I found that their intentions—expressed either emotionally, experientially, or objectively—were present as frameworks for the more detailed construction of the domains.

Gerald Edelman takes a more pragmatic approach to weaving intentionality into his theories of consciousness. Intentionality is bound up with the idea that awareness always has an object—that is, when we are aware, there is some *thing* of which we are aware. In other words, awareness always refers to something. That something can be a physical object that is before our eyes, such as a book; or something mental, such as the image of a past experience; or an abstract idea of intangible emotions and experiences, such as love or hate. For Edelman, this ability to refer to physical and mental objects is a prerequisite for higher-order consciousness and is one of the defining characteristics of human beings. It is, he maintains, biological and hence evolutionary. After making the point that human awareness always has an object, Edelman goes on to contend that humans always show *intentions* toward these objects of awareness, through conscious acts or through events bound to individual will and choice. Consciousness itself, says Edelman, shows intentionality; it is of or about things or events. It is also, to some extent, bound up with volition. By volition, Edelman means not only choice but will, the command of choice.[9]

Edelman's purpose is not only to propose a physical realm in which we have intentionality toward concrete objects or images, but also to lay a scientific foundation for the ideas presented by early phenomenologists like Brentano and Husserl. To do so, he first must answer the question of whether or not a world of objects exists outside the mind. He goes about this task like a typical pragmatist, believing that there obviously is a world out there! Humans, he maintains, possess the ability to abstract—that is, to refer to and speak about the objects and experiences of the world without their actually being present. Humans construct their *intentions* toward those objects and experiences by interacting with the world and with other humans. They then *reconstruct* and *reorder* those intentions in the realm of remembrance.

I introduce the concept of "intentionality" because it illuminates so well the meaning, purpose, and will that underlie the sortings performed by the architects and architecture students in my research. When asked to pick a meaningful theme that would explain the importance of their remembered places, these themes were expressed in three ways: emotionally, experientially, and objectively. These denotations reveal the underlying intent each participant has towards the content of each sort. In other words, while each individual sorting gave me the significant form of the memories—i.e., secret place, hidden place, shared space, etc., the description and intent of each sort were either emotionally charged, experientially felt, or objectively abstracted.

We are left with the question of *how* a designer understands the significance of a past place experience as it is applied to the act of design. My research suggests that, when presented with a design task, designers remember past places through a filter of emotion, they imaginatively reexperience them, or they remain objective about their content; that is, they display purposeful and calculated intentions toward their own remembered places as they may apply to a future place. Remembrance itself is an act of becoming conscious of some past experience. Images of place or their abstractions are "objects" of our consciousness; we become directed toward them. Remembrance is an *intentional* act. It bestows meaning—our intention—through an emotional, experiential, or objective framework and through combina-

Intentional Frameworks

tions thereof. The act of remembrance "filters" the memorable place according to our intentions toward the remembered place in the context of a new design.[10]

It should also be noted that designers displayed a fluidity across domains as they assigned each image to different categories. At the same time, they shifted from one intention to another, depending on the content of the meaning they were trying to communicate. When they sorted their memorable places along the lines of intimacy, self-awareness, or inner comfort, they were conveying emotional intentions toward their own memories of place. Yet another sorting by the same person would categorize the same set of memorable places according to sensory concerns, social interaction, or a stage of life; these were deemed to convey an experiential intention toward these memories. Objective intentions were clearly evident when the designers removed both their sensations and their emotions from the content of the sorting and concluded that physical properties or typologies of place were important to the memorable place experiences. Since the designers I interviewed moved from one intention to another during the average of three to four sortings, I have concluded that designers are capable of moving place images across domains, based on a particular circumstance for framing the memory. Furthermore, they can change their intentions, consciously or subconsciously, depending upon their immediate purpose or context. I am confident that what occurs during design is clearly related to a designer's intentionality in introducing a particular memory or domain in addressing his or her task. Domains, with their obvious content-laden meaning, certainly have purpose in framing design inquiry and testing design potential. In addition, I am suggesting that intentionality is the designer's purposeful (perhaps willful) attention to the reason a particular image or domain might be useful (i.e., what the designer intends emotionally, experientially, and/or objectively) in the act of design.

INDULGING THE SELF: EMOTIONALLY CHARGED IMAGERY

The term *emotional intention* denotes the personal references that individuals make to physical or mental objects in an internal, sympathetic, sentimental, or passionate manner. When designers referred to a memorable places, the references expressed a form of personal meaning. They responded to the remembered place or set of places with feeling. Designers expressed these emotional intentions in such phrases as "places that bring me closer to my higher self"; "places that surround myself in time"; "places I construct in dreams of self"; "places which evoke mysticism in me." These titles present descriptions of places as being either empathic or valued as an internal, self-oriented framework.

In the essays written by designers who participated in the Spatial Solitaire game, several references were made to the emotional content of either remembering or the place remembered. Mark Moreno describes a childhood porch in terms of his own identity:

> The discovery came by taking this sketch as a challenge to revisit a memory which I feared would produce unknown evils. In the process, it became evident and significant that I was always alone in my memories of the porch. This is ironic, because I have seven brothers and sisters, and the house was relatively small. I discovered that part of my identity lay in the meaning of the porch, for, as soon as I opened the door, I would cease to be an individual. The porch consequently always represents a place of security. It gives me the ability, the confidence, and the freedom to distinguish myself from my siblings.
>
> It is here that I really begin to understand my own inclination to associate or identify with the elements of the design world. I have a tendency to personify the elements of design. To explore the relationships of the elements as if they have personalities is to have empathy for them, in that I can understand their immediate needs in a given context. (Appendix 4)

Mark is empathic, identifying with a particular place of realization. The designers who shared their memory banks spoke of such places and valued them as they valued their own identity and the insights that had occurred to them in place. We all seem to have those "moments of being" that are necessary to our existence within the surround of "others."

One of the passages from literature that most clearly addresses an emotional response to place occurs in Proust's *Swann's Way*, in which he describes how he frequently woke in the middle of the night and felt unsure of where he was. The passage depicts his thoughts upon waking:

> These shifting and confused gusts of memory never lasted for more than a few seconds; it often happened that, in my spell of uncertainty as to where I was, I did not distinguish the successive theories of which that uncertainty was composed, any more than, when we watch a horse running, we isolate the successive positions of its body as they appear upon a bioscope. But I had seen first one and then another of the rooms in which I had slept during my life, and in the end I would revisit them all

*Intentional
Frameworks*

in the long course of my waking dream: rooms in winter: where on going to bed I would at once bury my head in a nest, built up out of the most diverse materials, the corner of my pillow, the top of my blankets, a piece of shawl, the edge of my bed, and a copy of an evening paper, all of which things I would contrive, with the infinite patience of birds building their nests, to cement into one whole; rooms where, in a keen frost, I would feel the satisfaction of being shut in from the outer world (like a sea-swallow which builds at the end of a dark tunnel and is kept warm by the surrounding earth), and where, the fire keeping in all night, I would sleep wrapped up, as it were, in a great cloak of snug and savory air, shot with the glow of the logs which would break out again in flame: in a sort of alcove without walls, a cave of warmth dug out of the heart of the room itself, a zone of heat whose boundaries were constantly shifting and altering in temperature as gusts of air ran across the floor to strike freshly upon my face, from the corners of the room, or from parts near the window or far from the fireplace which had therefore remained cold.[11]

This emotional identification with "nesting" often was conveyed as designers sorted their remembered experiences under categories that translated into "intimate" or "comforting" places. The scale was small and personal. The act of nesting is familiar to designers, and they recognize its emotional dimension in other depictions of place (the tree house is a good example). To use a powerful image like this in design and transfer its emotional charge to a future place, the designer must "feel" its force and portray this intention in such a way that it survives the design process and is reintroduced in a place that captures the potential for nesting and its emotional dimension.

Some of the issues designers cite as important and identify with an emotional response are similar to those which are grouped as being experiential in nature. I found that designers' intentions toward comfort, intimacy, and privacy can be understood as both emotional and experiential. The distinction between the two rests on whether the intention or response was organized around the internal, feelingful self or was a depiction of the characteristics of a place. If the domain indicated that issues of comfort or intimacy originated within the designer, then the intention was emotional. Examples of this type of reference included "I was comforted by the place," "I felt comfortable," and "These places evoke intimacy for me." If the response was framed in a way that attributes comfort and intimacy to the physicality of individual places, it was judged to be a less empathic intention; rather, the remembrance was more experiential in nature. Examples of experiential intentions include phrases and depiction such as "This place is soft and comfortable," "The color of this place is exciting," and "I remember this place as simple and elegant."

Some theorists might conclude that the process of "indulging the self" that is evident in the designers I talked to is the very bugaboo that architects have been trying to avoid for the last fifty or so years. However, I am suggesting that the nature of human "being" cannot be otherwise. We come to "know" about places through emotional intentions, as well as experiential and objective ones, *because* we are human and *because* these dimensions of knowing are all we have. So, when we are put in the position of creating new places, our intentions toward the unknown in the design task in front of us often are framed by the places we know and our basic understanding of our own life-world and how that complex conception relates to the life-worlds of others. The Howard Rourke syndrome—based on Ayn Rand's caricature of the egomaniacal "suffering artist"—is, of course, justifiably deplored, but it is an extreme and instrumental version of what I am discussing here. I have found that focusing on shared experiences and empathic understanding is the only way we can provide a future full of places that are both meaningful and fulfilling; moreover, this can occur without falling into megalomania.

EXTENDING THE BODY: EXPERIENTIALLY FELT IMAGERY

Experiential intentions are those that involve active body-memory constructions, event experiences, and significance in conjunction with a sensate experience. Experiences related to moments in time or to benchmarks of personal history were cited by designers and also are viewed here as experiential intentions. Further, even social interaction—our experience of being with others in places—helped the designer to form experiential intentions by using mental imagery of those situations and was considered experiential in nature. Shared or social experiences of place took on more significance for designers as they matured past their college years and became more attuned to those human needs and desires for contact.

Experiential intentions include a full range of qualitative attributes and sensate responses. Designers often frame their immediate design tasks through constructs that describe memorable places as having qualities of light, texture, color, or other qualities, such as comfort or intimacy. Examples of sensate intentions are found in such phrases as "The light is strong and powerful in these places," "The texture of materials in these places is fine," "These are gray and black places." Other attributes judged by the designers to be experiential were the power or strength of the memory, its influence in the individual's life, or whether the individual learned some lesson from the place.

Intentional Frameworks

97

Aldo Rossi's *A Scientific Autobiography* offers an example of sensory experience being clearly conveyed:

The façade of Las Pelayas is one of the masterworks of seventeenth-century Spanish architecture, and it had always made such a strong impression on me that Catalan friends, in one of their publications, treated it as an image analogous to my building in the Gallaratese quarter of Milan. There, in the interior of the cells, I noted a striking luminosity which contradicted the nearly prison-like aspect of the exterior façade. The same shouts that reached the outside of the convent were perceived on the inside with even greater sharpness, as in a theater. In the same way, the young man's eyes perceive the sights of the exterior as in a theater, or as one who watches a performance.[12]

In 1985, Barton Myers described his vision of desert and courtyard architecture to a design jury in Phoenix, explaining its applicability to the Municipal Center buildings he was proposing:

In this culture of the desert, the tradition of the wall, the earth color, . . . [convey] coming to grips with how to make shade. This (slide) is a fabulous building by Sir Edward Lutyens in New Delhi, and the cornices . . . give you the sense of trying to make the buildings cool. When the sun angle is 90 degrees, that top cornice will . . . [protect] the wall [from the direct sunlight]. So that when you look at these buildings, they don't look like they are sitting in the sun of 115 degrees and their wall temperatures would be 150–170. They look like they are responding and being cooled . . . There is a degree of scale, but the Arabs know very beautifully how to make hard paved courts which are beautiful oases with only a little bit of water and almost no planting (slide of Middle East courtyard). There are lessons to be learned, and certainly the cooling of the arcades is a lesson from that one. The possibility of the oasis within the wall, small gardens, smaller planting areas, wherein you have water, use it for irrigation system in a very sensitive way. Interesting in these kinds of cultures is the length between street and court. This [slide] is a beautiful example of [Las] Ramblas in Barcelona, which is one of the great pedestrian promenades in the world, and always the relationship of street to court, and that is something that interests us in this scheme.[13]

These accounts provide vivid depictions of designers who were not simply defending positions with after-the-fact examples, but rather were rehearsing a set of images to which they referred in order to share the meanings they intended to convey with their particular designs. In essence, the designers were revealing how they conceptualized their initial ideas of what the buildings and their surroundings should be like. Architects have rich and sensuous stockpiles of places from which they mine ideas that they creatively reconstruct and reinvent for present design situations. Obviously, designers rely on important constructions of memorable places as fuel for ideas and manipulations during the design act, as well as employing them to convince clients of their intentions.

When the designers' central concern is people and activities rather than place, they consider the experience to be one of social interaction. Grouped with this construct are considerations such as with whom the designers experienced the place, the activities they named, and the kinds of interaction they could have there with other people. Often these "social" images are fused with place, as both are juggled and intertwined.

In Mark Lochrin's description of the game of Spatial Solitaire (see appendix 15), the "act" that Bugs is involved in is one of "negotiation." This activity is decidedly social, and sometimes adversarial, and begins to suggest that a social *pattern* of exposure and enclosure is what is needed. This is found in the context of interaction—the import of which is the social desire for give and take, interaction, and connection.

Aldo Rossi provides an example of a socially centered architecture as a cultural device that leads him to related memories:

> I perceived that I had simply recounted—in architecture and in writings—my impressions on a certain morning when I read the newspaper in the great *Lichthof* of the University of Zurich, whose roof resembles, unless I am mistaken, the pyramidal roof of the *Kunsthaus*. The *Lichthof* is a place that is very dear to me. Now, because of my interest in this place, I asked Heinrich Helfenstein to photograph the interior, which is always full of students from the ground floor up through the successive levels. And what was undoubtedly a university I saw as a bazaar, teeming with life, as a public building or ancient bath.
>
> Helfenstein took some very beautiful photographs of the *Lichthof,* but, unlike my account of that place, his unique sensibility led him to take them during a holiday. In these photographs, the luminous court and the aerial galleries are absolutely empty, the building is uninhabited, and it is even difficult to comprehend how it might be inhabited. In fact, Helfenstein refused to represent either the purity or the life of the *Lichthof.* He caught its potential for being lived in. These photographs *suspended*

Intentional Frameworks

the life which the building could contain, and only by observing this suspension did I clearly see the palm trees in the glass-walled court, thus associating all this with the notion of a greenhouse, an enormous *Palmenhaus;* I connected the university with the Invernadero at Barcelona and with the gardens at Seville and Ferrara, where I experience a peace that is nearly complete.[14]

As architects typically do, Rossi relates his memory first to his experience of the place as teeming, full of life, close with people. He then proceeds, through the eyes of a photographer, to reveal a different set of concerns. Both lead to other similar places that have a different intention altogether—peace, quiet, and clarity. The architects interviewed about their design process relied most heavily upon the experiential intention they displayed when contemplating the meaning of their own image bank.

REMOVING THE SELF: OBJECTIVE ABSTRACTION

Objective intentions emerge out of a more abstract, intellectual, and external response to the significance of places. Constructs aligned with this intention include the physical properties of places and place types. The physical properties include such things as scale, detail, geometry, organization, degree of enclosure, and juxtapositions of form and space. Here the designers did not concern themselves with describing places in terms of how they felt about them or experienced them. Rather, they removed themselves from these places in order to provide distanced intellectual analyses and relatively objective descriptions of their memorable attributes. Even the language was more analytical, reflecting the vocabulary of formal design. Examples included "These places are centrally organized," "These places are all related to water," "These places are loosely enclosed," "These are large-scale places," and "Detail in these places is the most important attribute." This objective stance also characterized the typologies constructed by the designers—the descriptive elements of functional realms that manifest as rules or as elements during design and are transformed into taxonomies, or rules of assembly.

My view is that this kind of intention is learned, in contrast to the other two, which are absorbed through "being" human. All students of design receive an analytical education. During professional training, they often learn to remove messy emotions and experiential content from their accounts and to survey a place dispassionately. There are enormous benefits to be derived from abstracting the objective criteria of places. For one thing, they are useful as a shorthand way of categorizing facts that might exist in the mind concerning memorable places. Of course, in the memory of place, facts other than attributes and type are difficult to maintain with any degree of accuracy. Qualities that change with time—scale, juxtaposition, geometry, etc.—are less tractable as time progresses and as images adjust to present needs.

DETERMINING INTENTIONS

Just as the designers could recall each place image through different domains, each domain can be realized through an emotive, experiential, or objective intention. Our intentions change according to need and desire. Each image, like a chameleon, could adjust to a designer's intentions, depending upon his or her situation and context. Intentionality is one of the keys to understanding the range of concerns any one image may present for the same individual at different times and under different circumstances. At one point, a designer may remember a hometown or backyard tree house as fond memories with personal implications. At other times, those same images may be mined for any objective, experiential, or emotive attributes the designer could apply to a design. This fluidity seems to come with some design maturity, and such development may account for the complexity of the changing values exhibited by student groups compared to practitioners across time, across circumstances, and along a conceptual lifetime.[15]

Mark Lochrin observes, "However, some of the more creative work I have seen among students seems to stem from a conscious attempt to mentally re-image a situation, in the depth of its physical attributes, such as feeling the brush of the clothes on the clothesline. This is a relatively rare act of imagination, often in an unconstrained moment, i.e., when at the drawing board. Usually, in people with an otherwise developed spatial sense and adroitness at composition, the present and convention crowd in before the lyrical past is heard" (appendix 15).

It is remarkable how evenly the use of place images through emotional, experiential, and objective intentions is distributed between students exiting professional education and practitioners. Exiting students and professionals differed only slightly in identifying their overall intentions toward their memorable imagery as the latter is applied to design. In general, this suggests that, although objective constructs are tools for making places, emotionally charged and experientially felt imagery also plays a critical part in presenting the content of conjectures made during design inquiry. Educational institutions may

Intentional Frameworks

be limiting students unnecessarily if they cause them to ignore or deny emotional and experiential memories of place in the act of design. The elasticity of an image seems to stretch across all frameworks, perhaps with different degrees of significance for the individual or with dynamic adjustments depending upon time, place, or purpose.

Perhaps younger students, whose objective intentions were, in many cases, stronger than those of the professionals, believed that the information contained in the objective constructs was what they were expected to learn while in professional education, no matter how informal or personal the memorable place images within their image banks. Students trained in a program that emphasized analytical and objective thought appeared to present more abstract responses about the meaning of place experiences. Since they were being bombarded with formal imagery (as they should be) and were being introduced to a new abstract vocabulary of analysis, it is not surprising that beginning students believe they should analyze all their experiences in this new, "professional," and objective way.[16]

The maturity of the student population, the length of programs, and the world view espoused by the programs account for some of the differences among students that were observed in the results. If the institution retains control of the student for a long period of time and reinforces abstraction as well as "timeless" principles and impersonal perceptual theories (such as Gestalt principles), the students may be less likely to value the emotive and experiential importance of past experience. Instead, the student is likely to imagine that the important things about place experience are the intellectual moves and objective attributes which can be derived from physical places. To some extent, the institution which educates students for longer intervals substantially influences, for the period of time the students are at that institution, the way students measure the meaning of their own place experiences. This is the intention toward memorable places that is generally encouraged as "designerly." However, as time passes, designers who were educated in such programs seem to regain more balance in the intentions they report concerning their memorable places, so that these places are allowed to occupy different positions on different design occasions. The three intentional frameworks of remembrance, with their overlapping domains, could allow for the internal adjustments, juxtapositions of information within the image, and manipulation of meaning which occur in the designer's thought processes. Intentionality also allows for the external adjustments which designers could make when applying an image to design projects. In fact, the strength of design may depend upon a designer's capacity to flex and manipulate her or his intentions to extract needed information. The "stretching out" toward the memorable image, the capturing of its meaning within familiar forms, and the ability to adjust intentionality toward this object—all these center designers in a milieu where choices are made through the appreciation of the knowledge and insight they have gained from past place experience.

Intentional
Frameworks

Chapter 6

Imagination and Innovation

I N AN ADDITIONAL SERIES of interviews with architects and graduate students, we reviewed the drawings, models, specifications, etc., that each had developed for a particular project. From these materials we generated an account of the images and ideas that each designer remembered using during the design process. After having each designer sort these ideas and images, I concluded that they fell into six very basic categories. *Specific places* are places that are named and identified in time and space. *Specific events* are occasions that are named and identified in time and space. *Scripted behavior* is behavior that follows known expectations and is schematically stored. *Place types* are groups of buildings that are defined by form, function, or content. *Schematic configurations* are abstracted schemata, based upon function or behavior that results in a *gestalt*. Finally, there are *rational/geometric exercises,* in which logical "systems" are applied to convey order and significance.

Most of my previous research had focused on specific places and events. As I have noted, however, abstract principles of space, order, form, and behavior are introduced during design education and play a role in expanding the usefulness of specific places and events. At any rate, as designers engage in the act of designing, the furious movement of imagery between specific and more abstract knowledge is natural. The designer *must* have connections between these realms if anything at all is to be concluded in design. For example, one architect explained that he had carefully designed the fenestration of the house he was reviewing with me and seemed, to himself, somehow to be "wrapped up" in the proportioning of the windows and doors. He admitted that it was only after he had completed the design that he recognized that the source of his struggle for proportions was the image of his grandfather's barn and outbuildings. This architect, at this particular juncture, worked from abstracted schematics and geometry and then found his way back to a particular memory of a specific place. The same architect, on the other hand, had begun part of the project by utilizing some specific images of courtyard houses with which he was familiar and had abstracted schematic information from them.

Specific imagery and abstracted knowledge are tangled together, as they should be in an imaginative mind. Indeed, I am not so sure that this tangle needs to be "understood" outside its usefulness. The complexity of working back and forth between the known (what the designer has experienced in life) and the unknown (the task set before the designer) is not surprising in a puzzle-seeking, problem-solving tactic. Some designers may not even be aware of this dance. It is enough that the designer finds a way through the messiness of a design problem. This untold story or free-form dance, however, makes it difficult to "teach" the skill of moving among past, present, and future to find viable directions for exploration in design.

Steven Moore describes this dance in his essay explaining a designer's ruminations on memory and design. He divides his memorable image bank between two sources—a subjective source of "disconnected frames that emerge from personal history" and an objective source of "abstract structures that emerge from cultural tradition." In addition to these sources is a stockpile of "formal antecedents, or exemplars, that designers carry around in their heads—Palladio's Villa Rotunda, Kahn's Exeter Library, Le Corbusier's Villa Savoye, and countless other images that are the products of education." Steven explores the two sources, or what he calls "levels" of subjective and objective memory. In the particular example from the game of Spatial Solitaire presented here, Steven describes the mix of memory in a particular design project as phenomenological—that is, unexplainable in objective or logical terms: "I have absolutely no idea why I connected Martin Heidegger to a bicycle that I have not recalled for thirty-three years. Such speculation is, without the skills of Jungian analysis, not a very productive enterprise. It seems enough to appreciate the possible mysteries that the relation might bring forth—both about Heidegger as a referent and about myself as a designer" (Steven Moore, appendix 16).

INTERPRETATION

The act of aligning abstracted knowledge, or what Langer refers to as "logical forms," with actual experience is defined by her as *interpretation*. Langer suggests that the interpretation of an abstract form—concepts of pattern, structure, or organization—is a process of looking for the kinds of things to which a certain form belongs. The "things" this book addresses are memorable experiences of place and occasion; and, now, the additional abstracted knowledge of logical forms to which a designer generally is introduced during architectural education. Langer argues that our ability to identify many phenomena as exemplars of the same "logical form" makes it possible for us to control the incredible variation in our experiences. Domains have *significant* form as they relate places within a "living" functional realm. The abstract analysis that is introduced during architectural education creates *logical* form and relates places on a physical, abstract, and intellectual basis.

fig. 23. Philosopher's Home, by Steven Moore

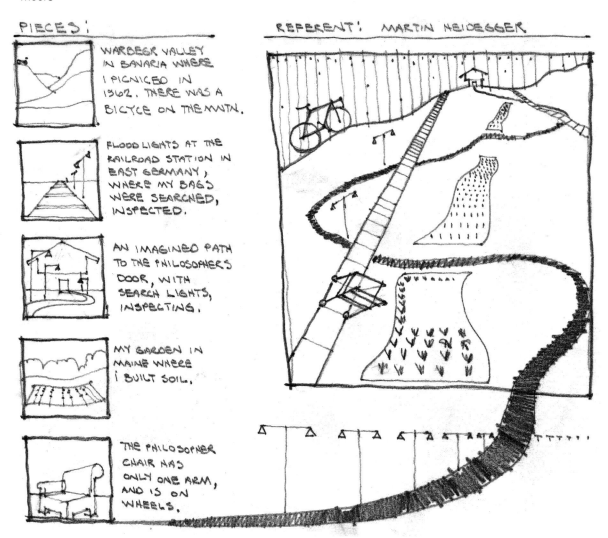

I recognized when making my drawing of the Philosopher's Home that I routinely experience two distinct levels of memory in the process of design. . . .

There is, of course, a tension between these two kinds of memory—the subjective and the objective, the local and the universal. The romantic favors the former, and the modern favors the latter. Rather than accept either of these exclusive possibilities, I struggle to find an inclusive memory that operates within both categories of recollection, that dwells exclusively in neither the local nor the universal. To do so, we need access to both levels of memory—to the bicycle on the mountain and the twenty-five-square plan that orders my drawing. (Steven Moore, appendix 16)

Julio Bermúdez designed a bridge across a river in his hometown of Santa Fe, Argentina, for his mother to use in walking while thinking. While he does not explain this particular act of interpretation in his essay concerning the game of Spatial Solitaire, he does explain the "essential nature of memory" as "initially perceptive because it is only by seeing something else that memory becomes operational and thus useful. Yet, as soon as this has occurred, the perceptive function switches to a procedural or behavioral function (way of doing)."

Human cognition and behavior are based upon our capacity to match new situations, problems, and solutions to those encountered earlier (i.e., recorded past experiences, knowledge). In other words, people learn from problems to see situations as like each other, as subject to the application of the same . . . law or law-sketch.[1] A particular mnemonic representation is applicable to a given situation because of certain features common to both that representation and the present experience. Analogies and inferences are the mental mechanisms used to make the necessary connection between the two. (Julio Bermúdez, appendix 17)

Interpretation begins with an abstraction (place type, properties of place, scripted behavior, schematic configuration, or rational/geometric exercise) and seeks some specific place or event that embodies it. Designers often summon an exemplar from their own experience to help structure a deeper understanding of abstract design ideas. All humans share this ability to transform an abstracted place type, schematic configuration, properties of place, or scripted behavior. Designers move back and forth between objectified schemata and concurrent memories of place as they proceed through design.

Imagination and Innovation

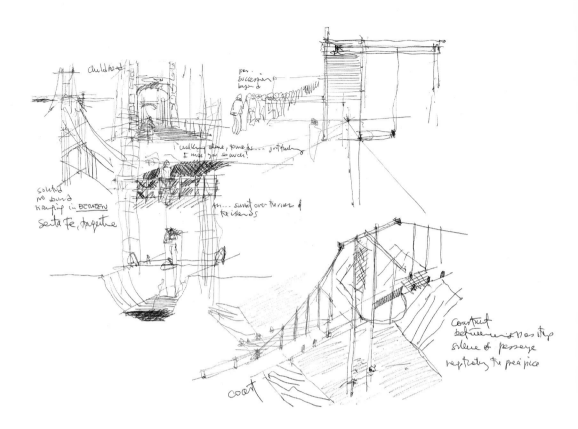

fig. 24. Mom, Walking While Thinking, by Julio Bermúdez, Assistant Professor of Architecture-University of Utah

There is no "correct" way for the designer to proceed. A designer could begin to think using one framework, then weave his or her way through related images in other domains, and eventually puzzle through to a useful end.

A participant in spatial solitare, Jef7rey Hildner, exemplifies in appendix 13 the unending process by which memory is invented and reinvented, how one idea chases another, and how formal design moves can create new avenues of exploration:

Figure|Field
> chess game (and sub-game) of inter-contingent fields and figures, sub-fields and subfigures, discontinuous and ambiguous figures . . .
> dissipation|concentration, extension|contraction, empty|full, center|edge, cut|intercut|countercut . . .
> *The Knights Move* (Shklovsky); *Violin* (Picasso), *papier colleé*, 1912 (cut, separate, shift, rotate)

Remembrance and the Design of Place

Roger Spears depicts this process in his essay "Stuff Shows Up": "The question of memory's utility to the designer is an intriguing one, though it might well be understood as something which too often is taken for granted—a kind of instinctive, unconscious reflex which generally just 'shows up' without deliberate or critical forethought. Which may be all for the best." He draws a colorful analogy between the act of design and hosting an elegant cocktail party. Sending invitations (dipping into memory) produces, along with the host's favorite people (memorable experiences), a few tedious acquaintances. But the setting also may be ripe for a party crasher—someone unexpected who gives the party life.

> The designer's use of memory is a bit like hosting an elegant cocktail party. You send out a slew of invitations, noting time, location, and some inkling of the purpose of the event, and then sit back and wait, not entirely sure of the response you will receive. To be sure, you can expect some old cronies to show up. Some trusted and familiar friends are welcome. Others, who arrive mostly out of a compelling sense of social obligation, are perhaps not so welcome. Either (or both, for that matter) offer an expected presence, be it reassuring or troubling, which nevertheless may also be tiresome, for you have seen all these people many times before and have grown ever so weary of their canned cocktail rap. You truly long for something new to stir things up this time around.
>
> Hopefully, somebody else (somebody unexpected) shows up: perhaps the companion of an invited guest; or a chance acquaintance you invited for a lark; or, best of all, a party crasher. The unexpected guest offers the opportunity for something new to occur: an interesting twist on a long-standing debate, a new and refreshing point of view or opinion, perhaps even a spirited though minor altercation among the players present.
>
> At least that's what you hope for: the convergence, on one particular evening, of the familiar and the unexpected, both coalescing to produce something unique or intriguing or, on a rare occasion, something absolutely spectacular. (Roger Spears, appendix 18)

My observations over years of research, teaching, and design suggest that two different approaches to design inquiry are intermingled. Designers can approach a project by utilizing either memorable mental images of place and occasion, or more abstract, schematic images garnered from specific places or occasions. I do not believe there is a preferred way to "begin" design—the process is too open-ended and depends upon people, time, site, politics, users, world affairs, and so on *ad infinitum*. However, I think the two different approaches are useful in very different ways. I suspect that the mappings

Imagination and Innovation

109

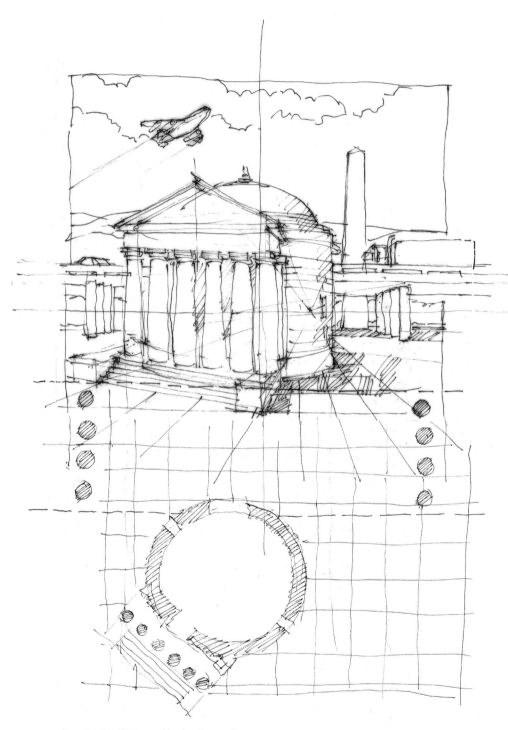

fig. 25. Stuff Shows Up, by Roger Spears

of abstract principles of behavior, properties, types, and schematics are rooted deeply in the brain. These represent "knowledge" that is reinforced over and over in the designer's experience. The designer does not have to contemplate their use in depth, because they are "known" abstractions. The decision to use an "axis down the middle" has such history and encompasses so much cultural and qualitative information in its embodied actions that the designer may not need to dwell on such a decision beyond its appropriateness to the task at hand. If the designer needs to contemplate whether it is appropriate, he or she "interprets" the abstracted information by remembering specific places or occasions that make the schematic information more experiential and/or emotional. As Steve Moore puts it in appendix 16, "Formal memory is not of personal history, nor of learned antecedents, but of Kantian categories—circles and squares, public and private, and so forth."

If, on the other hand, the designer begins with a specific place or occasion as a referent, it may be that the designer is unclear about its relationship to the task at hand, or that the task at hand triggers some past place or event experience that needs to be queried in depth before the designer's intentions become clear. This kind of beginning is definitely "messier" than a more abstract one, because the images are "full," complete, and whole. When the designer begins abstractly, for instance, he or she may not need to interpret an actual place or occasion to determine its "fit" with the new design task. If the designer begins with a complex, interwoven, and ever-changing image, however, he or she must contemplate its meaning and appropriateness from the opposite position.

The premise of this book is that, when an architectural designer collects and stores mental images in what this study defines as an image bank, those images constitute the basic building blocks for the design of future places. A mental image is the sensation of visual form and space, movement, sound, smell, or taste, captured and stored in the mind. This image may surface for moments of time. The mind can hold, or suspend in time, mental images from past experience; these the architectural designer uses as templates to test what a future place or experience might be like. In the designer's mind, past place imagery serves as raw data for imaginative conjectures made during the design process. Very little research has directly explored the nature of the mental image and its implications for use during the act of design. Delving into this condition could produce a useful, albeit messy, theory of memory and imagination.

Imagination and Innovation

This part of me remembers in one way and could go on for hours describing sensations. These memories would invariably lead to a nostalgic trip down "memory lane." However, the designer self (that is, the one with a background in design, who has a propensity for thinking and assimilating in a particular way and who has responsibilities and design intentions for the memories) already has begun prioritizing and analyzing associated words and phrases that have architectonic implications, i.e., Symbol, Public Mask, Threshold, Divider, Barrier, Gravity, Balance. This mental fork in the journey involves detaching from the memory and establishes a new agenda with a new kind of momentum. (Mark Moreno, appendix 4)

IMAGINATION

Imagination transformation, or metaphoric transformation, is an obvious and continuous feature of children's play. Anyone who watches children at play can observe the use of empty boxes as fantastic vehicles, the space under a table as a miniature house, and the tree house as a citadel. While engaged in this kind of play, children use found props and fill in the details through their own powers of imagination. Through their imagination, children transform themselves, objects, and social roles, while at the same time maintaining an awareness of their original identity and function. Children are capable of maintaining a clear relationship between engaging in make-believe play and, at the same time, expanding their own understandings of the physical properties of objects and social roles in reality. In other words, to a child, the box is still a box, but simultaneously it is a space ship in another time, place, and dimension. The child is aware of both reality and imaginative potential.[2]

"I personally subscribe to the constructivist or phenomenological hermeneutical school of thought," says Mark Lochrin in appendix 15, "which maintains that all learning is dependent upon remembered mental identities of things, and that these mental identities have overlapping characteristics and imprecise boundaries. That is to say, the stuff of memories is not fundamentally dependent upon words. This displacement and substitution of mental images, along with the ability to recall in physical detail the locus of past actions, appear to underpin creativity in design."

Remembrance and the Design of Place

Mental imagery lies at the heart of make-believe play. Make-believe play enhances the capacity to store and retrieve images that already have been formed, emphasizing the recombination and integration of stored imagery. The act of design requires an architectural designer to control and manipulate mental imagery in the same way children transform, visualize, and order it through their imaginations. In design, bridging from past place experiences to the shaping of an imagined future is similar to children's fantasy and make-believe play. It is through *imagination,* then, rather than simple memory images, that the designer must apply and test information. The ability to assess an image's applicability to a future place does not necessarily mean that the past place experience itself will be adjusted, although that is certainly possible or even probable. After all, if a child can imagine a box to be a car while maintaining a version of knowledge that includes the reality of the box, there is no reason to believe that a designer cannot also manipulate and adjust the image of a past place experience during design inquiry while simultaneously maintaining an independent, enduring version of it. However, no image remains unchanged—through time and circumstance, its "reality" may adjust, modified by the referrals made to it.

> I believe the creative element of memory is significant for the designer: it allows one to reach back into her own past and find those "perfect" places from which to work and toward which to strive. Since we cannot comprehend what we have never seen or experienced, we would be somewhat trapped without the stretching, mixing, editing, and modifying of our memories. Memory and imagination become intertwined to let us reach beyond the everyday toward those places that become more incredible and powerful over time. I believe good design is dependent upon creative memory, carefully drawing from and orchestrating pieces of our past to allow a meaningful place to emerge. Architecture becomes a composition of the designer's memories. (Karen Cordes Spence, appendix 2)

Susanne Langer states that metaphor is the force that drives new abstractions of ideas in either a discursive or a presentational form.[3] By and large, however, according to Lakoff and Johnson, metaphor has evoked only peripheral interest in formal Western philosophy. To elevate metaphoric thinking to a central position in any world view requires a rejection of objective or absolute truth. Lakoff and Johnson introduce metaphor into philosophy through what they call an experiential approach. In other words, their world view is based not on an abstract philosophical construction, but on human experience and action in the embodied world. In this view, as was noted in the chapter on intentionality, metaphor is pervasive in both language and thought. It comprises a conceptual system of biological categorization and therefore is central to everyday life. Lakoff and Johnson conclude that life is fundamentally metaphorical in nature and that its essence is understanding and experiencing one kind of thing in terms of another.[4]

Lakoff and Johnson propose that we make reference to our past both conceptually, through words or images, and actively, through behavior and experience. In the Western tradition, language is the most obvious source of metaphoric expression. Underlying discursive expression, however, is a thought process that is also metaphorical. Langer agrees that metaphor is not just a matter of language. We act according to the way we conceive things. We conceive things by recognizing and categorizing patterns. When we are confronted with something that does not specifically "fit" an existing categorization, we find a "like" referent—something similar to what we are experiencing. Then, from simple categories and the ability to comprehend relationships between similar and dissimilar phenomena, we build a complex conceptual system. However, Max Black states that, to discover and understand new ideas or to describe new concepts, we use metaphorical references to "bring two separate domains into cognitive and emotional relation by using language [or images] directly appropriate to the one as a lens for seeing the other; the implication, suggestions, and supporting values entwined with the literal use of the metaphorical expression enable us to see a new subject matter in a new way."[5] This process of active thinking allows humans to live in an open-ended environment, and lets designers either choose paths that lead them to tried and true design options—that is, prototypes—or seek new patterns, order, or spatial relations by using precedents.

> Memory is knowledge. Memory can be used to help simulate new situations by means of exemplars. Memory liberates and traps: it liberates by giving a framework for action, from which such action then may depart; it traps, as the framework may be so strong that it proves impossible to break free of it. Memory *is,* to an extent, the universe of discourse. It establishes the reference point from which criteria and exemplars are utilized to accept/reject/develop ideas. Memory structures and shapes our perception of reality. Memory is generated and generates (supports and is supported by) a set of social habits used in everyday life to ensure social interaction (predictability). A good design use of memory should avoid its direct, literal utilization; otherwise, the mind avoids inquiry and falls into mechanical, uncritical behavior and stereotypes. The problematization of memory is essential. One does it by de-framing the context of thought, so that memory has to be used in a different, indirect manner. Design, as a process of action/inquiry, develops a memory. (Julio Bermúdez, appendix 17)

It is clear that architectural designers, like everyone else, function through metaphorical thinking. Whether they are conscious of it or not, designers constantly refer to past place experiences in order to check the emotional, experiential, or objective aspects of current design tasks. The act of design inquiry requires a designer to contemplate the significance of a future place. A mental image may present itself to consciousness, or one may be recalled actively. The image rivets the designer's attention, triggering a process in which its significance is grasped through active, discerning imagination. A designer can utilize this natural process of imaginative metaphoric reference by referring to places, events, or actions from personal history that suggest either prototypes or precedents for the task at hand.

The designer's use of mental imagery and imagination to bridge time suggests that an elastic and multidimensional understanding of memorable place imagery is necessary to comprehend its functional characteristics. Seeing the future as an adjustment of the past, and seeing the past as an adjustment of the future both are very imaginative manipulations of memory by the designer. Remembered experiences have dimensions which suggest that designers can imaginatively manipulate and juxtapose objective, emotive, and experiential aspects within the concrete and realistic construction of the image. The designers I interviewed, no matter how well known, were by nature pragmatic and indicated that past place experience is *useful*. They were not shy about using whatever would help them order and solve complex and unwieldy design problems.

> The Rockefeller workshop sketches are influenced by my father, and by James Dine, Claus Oldenburg, and Julia Child as well. In the worlds of these workers, our understandings of tools are challenged. Dine fabricates and contorts his own tools; Oldenburg makes tools out of assorted materials and at megascales; Child—who presents herself as perfectly organized in her pegboarded workshop—uses the most wonderfully made devices to bring her great creations to life.
>
> In the sketching exercise, I drew upon memories of my father, of gallery exhibits done by Dine and Oldenburg, and of Child's WGBH television show to visualize the hypothetical workshop of Rockefeller 3rd. The tools became dominant, essential, organized, clean, as does the small building that is the workshop; clean lines, the pegboard grid enlarged to determine wall locations, the edges of benches, and the like. (Wes Janz, appendix 3)

PROTOTYPES AND PRECEDENTS

Mental images of memorable places, whether their sources are specific places, specific events, scripted behavior, place types, properties of place, schematic configurations, or rational/geometric exercises, present themselves in the designer's mind as experiences and knowledge to be mined for their significance to a present task. Designers use memories as conjectures for design by referencing image to task through the use of two constructs: prototype and precedent. These two types of referents allow designers to make conjectures—to compare and contrast information, feeling, or sensation derived from past experience to an unfocused design task at hand. Each memorable mental image of place or occasion can be thought of as belonging to a range of domains, and can be applied to design through a range of intentions. This is probably as far as we can proceed without getting desperately lost inside imaginative thinking.

A *prototype* is defined here as the first or primary type of something, to which a derivative conforms or is required to conform; it is a pattern, model, standard, exemplar, or archetype.[6] This definition is reiterated in various forms in the architectural literature as a set of places that are linked functionally or formally in a group, typology, or taxonomy.[7] Some clarification is necessary here in order to prevent the reader from confusing prototypes with a simpler term, *typology.* Edelman states that typologies are destroyed by evolution.[8] By this he means that a typology—in the classical definition, a very simple categorization by "type" or "kind"—is a myth. The world is a changing, surging, seething, open-ended environment in which types do not survive for long. While complex experiences must be rationalized, one order, whether historical, geological, or psychological, can be upset by another. I use the term *prototype,* therefore, to define a typological "source" rather than an absolute type. Prototypes are loose categorizations that evolve with time. Architectural prototypes are the necessary boundaries we create and reconstruct to stay sane yet imaginative. They exist within complexity but can exist only in the limited space of a moment.

In Donna Kacmar's words, "What is useful is to study the power in memory and recognition. Often designers will create something, only to discover later the object's similarity to something else. Was the designer copying? Did the designer only forget something from his memory? How is it significant that the new object triggers an old memory? Is it?" (appendix 6).

To use a prototype as a template to "see" a future place is a strategy for comparing "like" phenomena. The most common reference for an architect to make is to compare a particular project to past projects of the same functional or physical type. If an elementary school is being designed, for example, the initial inquiry could involve comparing the task to elementary schools that the designer remembers or buildings related to elementary schools, or exemplars found through research. Prototypes in design are equivalent to analogies in language, thought, and experience. An analogy is a referent that compares items which are more similar than dissimilar. At the opposite end of what some theorists refer to as a continuum[9] is the metaphor, a referent that compares items which are more dissimilar than similar. Metaphors in language, thought, and experience are equivalent to precedents in design. Julio Bermúdez puts it this way: "The socially approved way of utilizing memory in design is through the use of precedents implying the continuity/critique of a language and typology. Memory is a constructive process/product. It is interfacial: both subjective and objective." (appendix 17).

Precedent is defined here as a previous instance or case which is, or may be, taken as an example or rule for subsequent cases.[10] To use a precedent as a template to envision a future place is defined here as a strategy of comparing atypical phenomena. Precedents can be built places that are not prototypically related to the task at hand. Precedents also can be derived from natural forms, objects, or abstracted social situations. A designer is free to conjecture that an elementary school is somehow a tree house, an African village, or a marketplace. In the act of making references between precedent and future place, the designer identifies some kinship—a relationship discovered in form, space, order, or behavior—that presents design directions to be explored. As Langer suggests, these referents present different "contents" that may display some underlying, shared logical form.[11]

Scott Wall explores such concerns in appendix 11: "In those shadowed interiors and infinite transgressions of space, filled with implements of torture, or instruments of scale and measure, or the mechanisms of construction, I found a dense, palpable ambiguity which denied closure, which questioned the singularity of form. Eisenstein, Yourcenar, Robbe-Grillet, and Tafuri traversed this territory, exploring the intertwining immediacy of form and content, making indistinguishable the boundaries between drawing, thinking, and meaning in the simultaneity of Piranesi's spaces."

Next let us turn to a project by Kallman, McKinnell and Woods, published several years ago in *Architectural Record*.[12] This project is a useful example of working with both prototype and precedent, because the designers invested the time and effort required to record various images and ideas they used in designing the American Academy of Arts and Sciences. The images address site, themes of significance, and pragmatic requirements.

The existing hilltop is transformed into a building that continues its pyramidal peak in a clearly metaphorical reference. It is the reference between the pyramid of the hillside and the resulting pyramidal form of the building that forms the logical connection between two dissimilar references—the shape of earth becoming the precedent for the resultant response of the

Imagination and Innovation

117

building. The logic is very similar to that used in the next image, introduced simply as "Shady Hill." Essentially, the implication is that the building must continue the site condition of "shade" by extending the overhangs of the pyramidal roof and by supporting these overhangs with brackets. Both the shady overhangs and the brackets are suggestive of a building sitting comfortably among trees, as the precedent suggests.

Before I proceed, I must explain that, although these images are introduced in the original publication (and here as well) as having a sequence, I believe this perception is false. Images rarely come into use in a linear stream of thought. As presented in *Architectural Record* and in this book, these images are prisoners of the logic of language that—in printed form at least—is necessarily sequential. In fact, these images and ideas are more likely to be intermixed and related, perhaps hermeneutically. That is to say, they present themselves as a constant weaving together of ideas, some occurring to the designer simultaneously, others arriving in a chain reaction, and still others sneaking into the process without the designer's being completely aware of their presence. So, as I discuss these images, the reader must imagine that the actual process is much messier than the eventual formal reconstruction suggests. This is an illustration of the inevitable struggle between imagery as it presents itself in the mind and the more sequential expression of the written word.

The third image introduced in the original *Architectural Record* article is "The Scholar Shaded." This image supplies and sustains a thematic construction that, in turn, describes how the designers understood the character of their clients. The "scholar," shaded and sheltered, is a *precedent.* This idealized figure reflects the designers' desire to capture the nature of exchange among scholars and fuse it with their conception of the site.

A fourth image collects several ideas and images. This particular drawing, I believe, is more indicative of thinking through some ideas. "The Paradisical Hut and the Tree House" are woven together as a combined image of philosophical retreat with physical structure. The tree house has the significant form of protection, privacy, and removal from the earthly plane; its logical form is suspension above the ground plane, bracketed reference to the larger structure, and filtered enclosure. The paradisical hut suggests that, as in original, ancient structures, the construction is evident and honest. These metaphoric references are precedents, sometimes holding in their expression a theme for the designers to utilize in making some physical decisions. The resulting built form must be an "honest" expression of materiality and its obvious structural capacities.

The fifth image, "A Classical Order," presents a more formal interpretation of the academy as an institution, one very unlike the earlier thematic

Shady Hill transformed.

fig. 26. Shady Hill Transformed, by Kallman, McKinnell, and Woods. Source: Mildred F. Schmertz, "A New 'House' for the American Academy of Arts and Sciences Designed by Kallmann, McKinnell and Wood," *Architectural Record* 11 (1981): 82.[n]

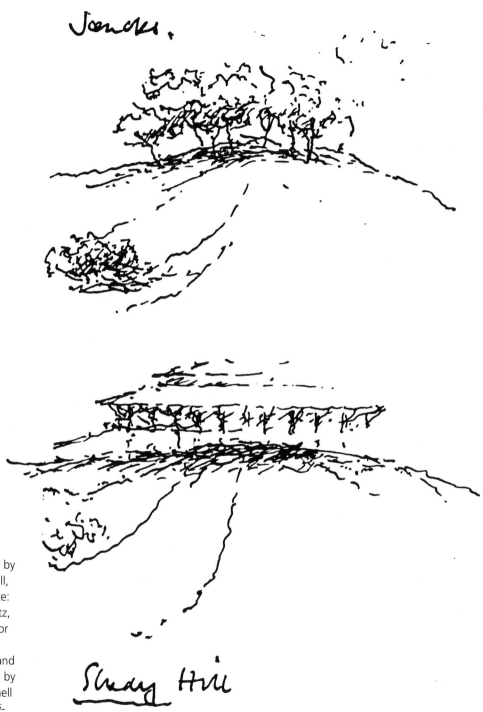

Jencks.

Shady Hill

fig. 27. Shady Hill, by Kallman, McKinnell, and Woods. Source: Mildred F. Schmertz, "A New 'House' for the American Academy of Arts and Sciences Designed by Kallmann, McKinnell and Wood," *Architectural Record* 11 (1981): 82.

The Scholar Shaded.

fig. 28. The Scholar Shaded, by Kallman, McKinnell, and Woods. Source: Mildred F. Schmertz, "A New 'House' for the American Academy of Arts and Sciences Designed by Kallmann, McKinnell and Wood," *Architectural Record* 11 (1981): 82.

notion of the individual scholar. This rigorous set of rules places the "group," or academy, of scholars within an "ordered" and institutionalized setting.

The sixth image, "The Hut Transformed," carries this abstracted and formal image even further by applying a geometry as a "learned" condition of proportion. The next two sketches tie the institution to the individual, as the ground-floor "shared" and formally proportioned elevations support the more individual tree houses of scholars above.

The joining of classical and "rude" is further supported by the addition of "Two Themes"—an image that expresses Classical and Romantic modes. These two themes capture the nature of the eternal and its opposite, an unavoidable process of decay to which all buildings are subject. This struggle is further elaborated in the depiction of Poussin's *Adoration of the Shepherds* as a dialogue. The architects use their experiences at "The Pazzi Chapel" to explore the rustic marriage of the temporal/temporary and the eternal. These

Imagination and Innovation

121

fig. 29. The Paradisical Hut and the Tree House, by Kallman, McKinnell, and Woods. Source: Mildred F. Schmertz, "A New 'House' for the American Academy of Arts and Sciences Designed by Kallmann, McKinnell and Wood," *Architectural Record* 11 (1981): 82.

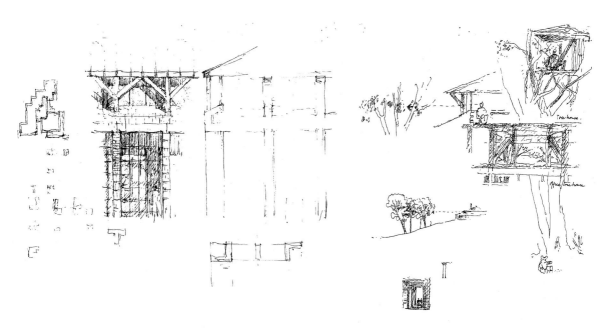

fig. 30. The Classical Order, by Kallman, McKinnell, and Woods. Source: Mildred F. Schmertz, "A New 'House' for the American Academy of Arts and Sciences Designed by Kallmann, McKinnell and Wood," *Architectural Record* 11 (1981): 83.

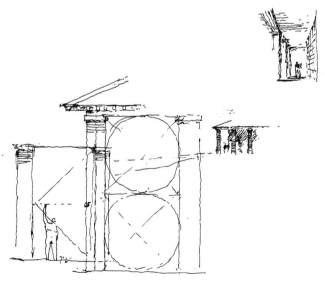

Rustic Temple fabrique / Brongniart 1783

fig. 31. The Hut Transformed, by Kallman, McKinnell, and Woods. Source: Mildred F. Schmertz, "A New 'House' for the American Academy of Arts and Sciences Designed by Kallmann, McKinnell and Wood," *Architectural Record* 11 (1981): 83.

123

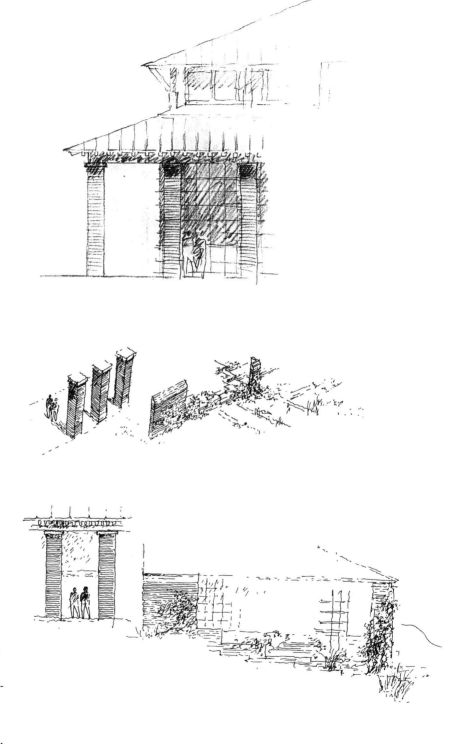

fig. 32. Two Themes, by Kallman, McKinnell, and Woods. Source: Mildred F. Schmertz, "A New 'House' for the American Academy of Arts and Sciences Designed by Kallmann, McKinnell and Wood," *Architectural Record* 11 (1981): 83.

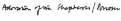

Adoration of the Shepherds / Poussin

Rebecca and Eliezer at the Well / Poussin

fig. 33. Poussin: Adoration of the Shepherds, by Kallman, McKinnell, and Woods. Source: Mildred F. Schmertz, "A New 'House' for the American Academy of Arts and Sciences Designed by Kallmann, McKinnell and Wood," *Architectural Record* 11 (1981): 83.

analogies for the juncture of opposing themes help the architects focus and convey the physical juncture of rustic and Classical in built form.

The final images are a mix of analogic and metaphoric referents. "The Amphitheater in a Room" uses the Teatro Olímpico to guide decisions concerning the programmatic use of a room for presentation and debate. The designers imagined the scholars in need of such a space at the American Academy of Arts and Sciences. They were not simply to "receive" information, as is true in a "lecture" setting. Rather, much as we imagine scholars doing in the time of Socrates, they would engage in debate and discussion that would not necessarily be contained within this one room. While debate was to be formalized, the room should be equalized between speaker and the audience.

Imagination and Innovation

125

Shelter over classical remains.

fig. 34. The Pazzi Chapel, by Kallman, McKinnell, and Woods. Source: Mildred F. Schmertz, "A New 'House' for the American Academy of Arts and Sciences Designed by Kallmann, McKinnell and Wood," *Architectural Record* 11 (1981): 84.

Moreover, this room that allows more organized debate also would encourage participants to spill out of it into other spaces for less public discussions.

The geometry of the amphitheater, as displayed in the plan, fits the orthogonal nature of "The House." In the plan, too, appears the *agora*—the atrium around which all rooms are organized. This agora brings the architects to their last metaphor, "The House as a City." Here are order and circumstance—the eternal Cartesian grid and the particular, contextual boundary; the orthogonal frame of the agora and the circular geometry of the theater. All opposing forces in plan, elevation, and section are drawn together into existence through the use of prototypes and precedents, in the process of transforming memory through imagination to create a future place.

126

While the definition of prototype and precedent may seem clear on paper, during the process of design inquiry, there are few "rules" or "definitions" that are consciously held. The distinction between these forms of conjecture gets blurred in the frenzy of design. A memorable place or event might be used as a prototypical template in one design circumstance and as a precedential template in another. The tree house, for instance, could be used as a *prototypical* template for a small frame structure that rests upon a more massive structure. Or the tree house might be used as a *precedential* template that helps the designer understand the desire for retreat. The classifications of

Gonzaga Theatre (Scamozzi).

Amphitheatre in a room.

fig. 35. The Amphitheater in a Room, by Kallman, McKinnell, and Woods. Source: Mildred F. Schmertz, "A New 'House' for the American Academy of Arts and Sciences Designed by Kallmann, McKinnell and Wood," *Architectural Record* 11 (1981): 84.

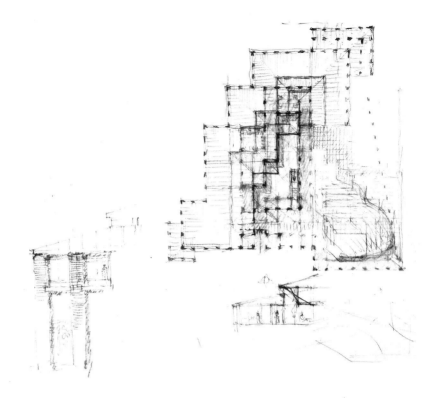

fig. 36. The Plan, by Kallman, McKinnell, and Woods. Source: Mildred F. Schmertz, "A New 'House' for the American Academy of Arts and Sciences Designed by Kallmann, McKinnell and Wood," *Architectural Record* 11 (1981): 84.

prototype and precedent have fuzzy edges and clearly can be twisted into many "deformities," as Rossi puts it.[13] The two strategies for comparing and contrasting mental images with a present design task are only clearly distinct as the poles on a continuum between similar and dissimilar referents.

MEMORY AND INNOVATION

Innovation in design is intimately tied to the manipulation of mental images. Because no experience is ever repeated exactly, the use of past knowledge to frame present or future situations necessarily demands abstraction, adjustment, and evolution of ideas, emotions, and experience derived from the past as these are applied to a possible future. Innovation refers to the amount of adjustment or manipulation necessary to bring ideas into alignment with the functions and intentions embedded in the present design situation. When a solution to a design problem resides within some knowledge of *similar* referents, the need for innovation is local; that is, it relates to the specifics of context, site, client, materials, etc. When a solution to a problem resides within some comparison of *dissimilar* referents, the need for in-

Remembrance and the Design of Place

novation is more global, because the two referents are related in a more complex way. Dissimilarity between past experience and a possible future raises more questions and demands a different kind of innovation if the two are to be held in conscious awareness at the same time.[14] The underlying space, form, order, or behavior then must be wrought from the inquiry itself and derived through a different kind of thinking. "Like the building of memories," Mark Moreno observes, "design is a process of assembly that seemingly has no definitive end. Even at the completion of any construction, designers are forever rethinking and redesigning. Our intellect and schedules, or our business senses, compel us to filter and distill seeds of design, choosing those that will serve us to a beneficial end" (appendix 4).

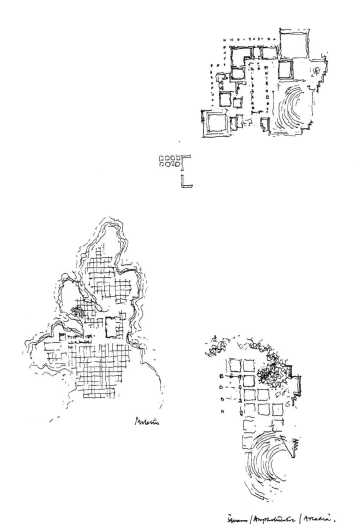

fig. 37. The House as City, by Kallman, McKinnell, and Woods. Source: Mildred F. Schmertz, "A New 'House' for the American Academy of Arts and Sciences Designed by Kallmann, McKinnell and Wood," *Architectural Record* 11 (1981): 85.

129

The measure of innovation required is its appropriateness to the task at hand. Using prototypes to make conjectures during design inquiry can be seen as generally maintaining a status quo, relegating innovation to smaller operations of adjustment and fit. Using precedents to make conjectures during design inquiry, however, requires a more extensive metaphoric conjunction and therefore a different innovative effort. The combination of known constructs not normally thought of as related can generate new perceptions, new relationships, and new problems. Because the metaphoric conjunction can cross modalities and features, as when death is compared to emptiness[15] or democracy to accessibility,[16] the opportunity for innovation through metaphoric precedent can lead to the rapid evolution of ideas. There are no rules for when, or under what conditions, prototypes and precedents should be applied to a particular design inquiry. It is a question of appropriate use that inevitably is tied to the character of a project and its contextual situation.

Chapter 7

Connections

M EMORIES OF PLACE connect meaning to the practice of architectural design, but where does this meaning reside? Is meaning inside us, does it reside within the objects we contemplate, or does it exist in some transactional relationship between us and the world? These are questions that occupy a philosopher. As designers, however, we act, we create, and we instruct others in how to make the places we design. We practice our discipline as best we can and make sense of it as we are able. Perhaps Langer gives those of us who care to understand these things the most promising answer when she alludes to the *utilitarian* doctrine of symbolism.[1] Our minds teem with daydreams, desire, fretful values, enthusiasms, fears, and awareness of "beyond" and of the "past." Langer believes it is the ongoing process of symbolization that is fundamentally rational—and essential—to thought. Our minds forge into meaning—into symbol—the material we humans encounter daily. Doing so is a requirement for our sanity. The process of ideation, the stream of symbols necessary to our continued existence, is a mental process that demands the immediate expression of meaning in the practice of our profession and in our daily lives. It is this very immediacy of mental imagery and its holistic presence that allow designers to build meaningful connections from past to future. As a result of the research summarized in this book, I can only conclude that memorable places are stored symbolically and transformed into meaningful domains as we recall them in conjunction with that which may be needed on our drawing boards. Because mental imagery is an act of holistic expression, and because we do not remember eidetically, the significance of the imagery connects the life lived in past experience to a potential future emotionally, experientially, and objectively, through the utilitarian act of design.

I believe the creative element of memory is significant for the designer: it allows one to reach back into her own past and find those "perfect" places from which to work and toward which to strive. Since we cannot comprehend what we have never seen or experienced, we would be somewhat trapped without the stretching, mixing, editing, and modifying of our memories. Memory and imagination become intertwined to let us reach beyond the everyday toward those places that become more incredible and powerful over time. I believe good design is dependent upon creative memory, carefully drawing from and orchestrating pieces of our past to allow a meaningful place to emerge. Architecture becomes a composition of the designer's memories. (Karen Cordes Spence, appendix 2)

If Kant is right, we can't help finding patterns in our world, because they emerge from the structure of our minds. I went looking for patterns in the information I elicited from designers, because I believe that, as humans, we live, communicate, and socialize as individuals and groups that are capable, if interested, in understanding other individuals or groups whose traditions and beliefs may be different from our own. It is the basis of that understanding, that connection, that is explored in these pages. Architectural designers are a breed, a group, who have the responsibility and the pleasure of making meaningful places. "It [the sketch] began with remembering and will not have an end. . . . " says Mark Moreno. "Memories, the makers of dreams, are powerful, sometimes elusive, and full of intrigue. They continually reconfigure that which makes personal identity. Consequently, memories and dreams are inextricably attached to what we, as designers, do" (appendix 4).

Gaston Bachelard claims that all great images have an oneiric depth—a place beyond consciousness. Memorable places seem to have seeds of symbolic meaning, complex and multidimensional, that present our connectedness—that seal our understandings of one another's experiences in this world. The dream-depth that Bachelard refers to is a phenomenological assertion of essence. However, phenomenologists seem to distill essence to one substantive theme. Perhaps that is an unfair statement, but I have never figured out whether essence is singular or plural in its intent. Is an essence a "thick" description of substantive material, or, as regards place, is it a singular spiritual sensibility? My work suggests layers, perhaps interwoven threads of meaning, a few of which grow denser at one juncture, then connect and grow at another juncture, depending upon circumstances in the remembered past, the tyrannical present, or the potential future.

I believe we as designers look to our memory and respond to it in our work. We respond not only to our personal memory but also to a more universal one—that memory which is learned as part of our historical and theoretical training. . . . We are reminded of our past, of the passing of time. We recognize the more universal aspects of life. Of course, the question needs to be asked: what is the purpose of architecture? Is it the place of architecture to remind people of their past? I think that it is. Architecture is an art, and the purpose of art is to reflect and ask for a response to this life condition. By provoking a memory or a series of remembrances, architecture is provoking a response to itself. It is referring to a life lived. Memory and architecture are irrevocably linked. (Donna Kacmar, appendix 6)

The places of our lives—the domains of memory—symbolize our human desire for contact, retreat, detachment, order, comfort, poetry, grace, freedom, solace, fear, and much more. These human characteristics are common to us all. They connect us as individuals, allow us to communicate; and their expression in architecture connects us to past places, present experience in place, and the potential future of places. Meaning seems to be reconstructed at the moment when memorable experience is united or merged with circumstances in the present. This architecture of shadows, of background, of meaning, is the designer's base of material through which connections are made and places are recreated.

Gaston Bachelard states, "Great images have both a history and a prehistory; they are always a blend of memory and legend, with the result that we never experience an image directly. Indeed, every great image has an unfathomable oneiric [dream] depth to which the personal past adds special color."[2] In a designer's special history of places exist images that have what Bachelard calls a prehistory—images that predate idiosyncratic experience and tie an individual to human history, the archetypal images that surface in folklore and legend. The term *legend* might be interchangeable with what Akhter Ahsen[3] terms *parables*. The parable is constituted of meaningful messages, encounters, or insights that are allegorical in nature; it teaches us something by its symbolic expression of life.

In more pragmatic terms, Edelman, in *Bright Air, Brilliant Fire*, presents a world view he calls "Qualified Realism," described as a "biologically based epistemology."[4] This view explains the phenomena of the "socially based individual." While in this world view categorization and metaphoric reference remain at the core of our abilities to order and imagine, real-world events are so "dense"—packed with emotional, experiential, and objective qualities—that it is impossible to exhaust all their descriptions. As humans, we follow these events through a myriad of individual sensations and perceptions that create unique paths of experience. The complexity of this jumble of paths often makes it seem that we have little in common with each other or with those of other cultures. Edelman's world view allows for an open-ended, indeterminate future, yet the very word *society* suggests that the "socially based individual" must possess the connections with other people that enable an individual to be social. It is the intermingling of these common experiences with the imagining of some form of future that allows humans to evolve and create. This, of course, begs the question of just what it is that is held in common and what parts of experiences are colored by individuality or socialization. One requires the other in a slowly evolving, culturally based, socially based, individual.

Edelman calls history a "flux of categorizations" within either primary or higher-order consciousness.[5] The flux of ever-evolving experience gives humans, with their higher-order consciousness, the ability to adjust and change through the open-ended criteria of categorizations that lead to metaphoric thinking and thence to adjustment. As humans, we are able to model the past and the future. These models flicker and change with events that impinge upon the individual in the present.

The question here, however, is whether the domains discovered from architects' sortings are classical—have immutable basic elements—or are more "loosely" organized, so that they fluctuate with changes in time, place, and circumstance. Edelman undoubtedly would choose the "loosely" ordered categories. Langer, too, agrees that the import of memorable imagery is never "fixed," that it has an ambivalence of meaning.[6] The research I report here also suggests a fluidity of meaning, a freedom of interpretation, and a blurring of time, as designers engage past experiences to operate within the present. It seems to me that all this is true.

I suspect, however, that there is something about the domains themselves that does not alter radically, or at least not rapidly. Perhaps what Bachelard refers to as *reverie* is the act of realigning individual experience to basic categories which are so critical to humans and define their humanity. This dance of relationships, associations, and linkages speaks to the connections among designers, connections to places they seek to design, and connections to the people, society, or culture for whom they design.

Elsewhere Bachelard states that reverie itself does not recount, but there exist reveries so deep that they go beyond individual experience. These reveries liberate us and return us to original solitudes.[7] He suggests that our childhood memories are not simply a reservoir of these original, essential experiences[8] (contact, retreat, order, grace, etc.), but also may be a conduit for an unfathomable depth of human existence. Underlying idiosyncratic experience, the human soul finds permanence—something that lies outside history. Reverie is one of the most important components of design—truly, it *is* the act of design, its creative formulation of, and connection to, significance. We "see significance *in* things long before we know what we are seeing."[9] What designers search for during their most profound reveries are reflections of human feelings and the sensuousness of life, power, and rhythm; and an order to space that will create a new place of significance. These things are hard to name. I believe their import is captured loosely within the domains of place and the significant reflections while "becoming" another place. This is one of the most difficult acts in design—the transformation of meaning, not in terms of logic but in terms of what is expressed and what is present. This is how connections to "others" are made—through artistic reverie, its labor of transformation, and the presentation of a new place full of recognizable life, a new place suffused with an unspoken idea.

Aldo Rossi has suggested that, as designers, we "transcend analogies" to achieve a process in which objects and places "evolve from one referent to another . . . melt and disappear during the process of becoming."[10] Perhaps this is a more poetic way of describing Edelman's open-ended process in which metaphors evolve from the known to help explain the unknown. Designers can be rational, in the sense that they are trying to "capture" the significant forms of past places and transform them into a future place. Langer, on the other hand, believes that this *technique* of transformation is the *means* to expressive form. A designer's technique of comparing and contrasting the past to the present and to an imagined future is one that should be encouraged and developed. It seems to be second nature—a shadowy background—for most designers, but transformation is an ability that students practice awkwardly as they glimpse its potential during their education. They are unable fully to grasp "transformation" until they deal with the profound complexity of making places. The artifact of design, the physical place, is a substantive combination of order, materials, and the intentions of the designer; it is the architects' practice, or art, to imagine the emergence of something more—something that can be called "the symbol of sentience."[11]

Connections

In everyday life, past experience helps us classify and categorize our incoming experience. During the act of design, however, designers must discover in their banks of knowledge and memory something that will *sustain* the process of design. The personal, emotional experience of revelation or insight is the mental atmosphere designers seek—a connection to meaningful ideas that will impact the process and carry them through to a successful end. However, designers often carry the energy of artistic labor beyond the end stage of a particular building. Ideas continue to evolve, giving us implicit understanding that inspires further investigation and expression. All the designer can hope for is that the unspoken idea of place is strong enough to be conveyed to others.

At times, designers sense a deeper concordance between their in-sights and the design task at hand and sense an import that is more profound than the project's stated purpose. These designers try to discover the project's potential by constructing its significance through domains that link memories of place to a possible future. They do this through the act of reverie, day-dreaming and designing with a bank of images that contains significant and recurring domains—the secret place, the Arcadian place, the ancestral place, the shared place, the alone place, the intimate place, the gregarious place, places that stretch to meet the horizon line, places that enclose and protect. These domains and others like them make it possible for designers to understand the significance of place and to communicate with both their clients and the people who will live, work, and play in the environments they design. Significant forms of life—contact, retreat, love, joy, fear, inadequacy, empathy, grace, intelligence, order, and many more—are available to designers and clients through the presentational form of their own past place experience remembered. It is the use of these images that allows architects to go beyond decorating buildings to discovering and working with significant form. Without this connection of the idiosyncratic histories of designers to the histories of others and to the human history of experiences, the act of design is empty.

Appendices

Client: An Institution
Place: The Parrot Stand

When I was growing up in Van Buren, Arkansas, one of our neighbors owned a parrot. On warm days she would move the parrot to the front porch, where he could observe the street and the passersby. On Sunday mornings, as we were going to church, the parrot would scream the word "hypocrite" at us. At first it seemed humorous, but soon I noticed that it seemed to make some of us uncomfortable. I asked my dad what the word meant. He explained that a hypocrite was someone who did not practice what he preached or thought. It had to do with integrity—in a person or even an institution. It seemed to me that any institution, including a university, should be reminded constantly to check its own integrity. Therefore, [I include] stations for parrots to scream out now and then the word "hypocrite" so that the institution might check itself.

Karen
Cordes Spence

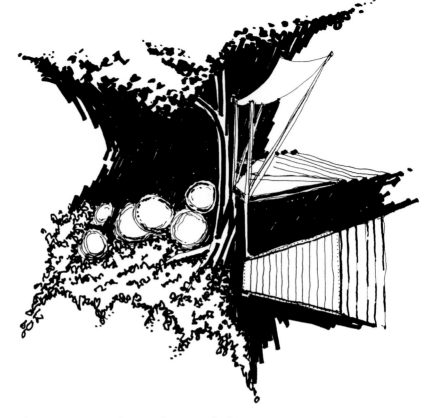

Character:	Dorothy in *The Wizard of Oz*
Act:	Being
Place:	Childhood Spaces

This place is for Dorothy in *The Wizard of Oz*. Dorothy is a strong character whom I remember from my childhood, an ordinary girl who had powers beyond her own recognition. The memorable elements that anchor this place for Dorothy are also from my childhood: the overgrown vines, the rocks, and the large oak trees provided an environment that I imagined as jungle trails, magnificent houses, boats, islands, treacherous roads, and infallible lookouts when I was young. My backyard had unlimited possibilities. The place for Dorothy begins from such unlimited possibilities (as all designs do), taking the shape of a simple wood structure that provides a space for many activities. It is a place to look, to sit, to imagine, to pretend, and to just be. It may be anything that one desires, like the elements in a childhood backyard. The wood structure is raised above the land to provide Dorothy with a view of the world around, yet it also has stairs to enable her to go wherever she chooses.

It is striking to find how creative our memories are when we return to remembered places. My husband and I both laughed when we returned to his childhood home to find the shed that he described as "at least twenty to twenty-five feet wide and a good forty or fifty feet long" to be no more than fourteen feet wide and twenty-four feet in length. It was equally amusing to visit the deep, dark forest with its gigantic rock formations in my childhood backyard and find only a few large shade trees with rocks that might measure four feet in diameter. I also have strong memories of the romantic forms of small Italian hill towns, the pristine and picturesque German villages, the colorful boisterous Italian festivals, the bizarre antics played out in Times Square, and the winds and the smell of rain on the Northwest Coast. These memorable events in my life seem to be wrapped with spaces, forms, and sense that seem to grow more defined, compelling, and sensuous over time.

I believe the creative element of memory is significant for the designer: it allows one to reach back into her own past and find those "perfect" places from which to work and toward which to strive. Since we cannot comprehend what we have never seen or experienced, we would be somewhat trapped without the stretching, mixing, editing, and modifying of our memories. Memory and imagination become intertwined to let us reach beyond the everyday toward those places that become more incredible and powerful over time. I believe good design is dependent upon creative memory, carefully drawing from and orchestrating pieces of our past to allow a meaningful place to emerge. Architecture becomes a composition of the designer's memories.

Karen Cordes Spence

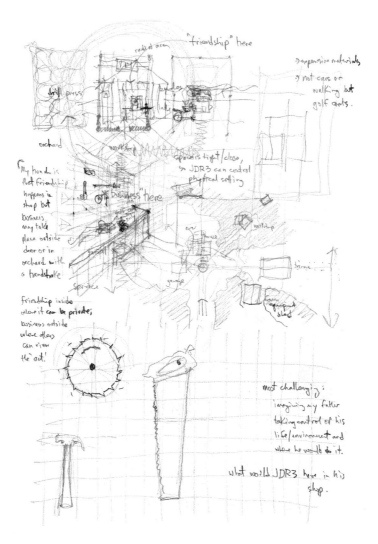

Client: John D. Rockefeller
Place: Father's Workshop

At the time of the conference [workshop, "Spatial Solitaire"], I was negoti-
ating my way through the doctoral program at the University of Michigan.
I was about to begin my written and oral examinations, which were to be
followed by the presentation of my dissertation proposal. Central to my project
was the need to understand better the inner workings of the elite group who
directed the design and construction of Lincoln Center for the Performing
Arts. The third John D. Rockefeller was essential to this nation-building
project.

    While in your session, I thought about Rockefeller as I knew my own father, Hersel Janz. Really, on some levels, the contrasts couldn't have been greater. Rockefeller: namesake of one of the richest men in the world, Princeton University alum, office in Rockefeller Center in midtown Manhattan, world traveler. Hersel Janz: grandson of an unknown immigrant to the United States, high-school dropout who would attain a high-school equivalency degree as an adult, farmer and factory worker who took one trip outside the United States.

I decided, however, to focus on how Rockefeller might relate to something my father did very well—work with his hands. As part of a larger residential complex that I sketched, I thought about the workshop a man like Rockefeller might design and maintain for himself in a secluded estate. To begin this process, I remembered my father's workshop that existed in our garage: pegboard with tools hanging askance; oil stains; peach crates filled with bags of nails, screws, and bolts; great drums of grease for the farm equipment; odd containers my father had collected from the factory in which he worked; a great vise; and the like. I also recalled my effort as a child to straighten up my father's workbench once while he was away. I reorganized, cleaned, swept, hung, threw out, and later came to realize that the new order I had created actually concealed most of the tools, because I had moved them from where my father knew them to be.

The Rockefeller workshop sketches are influenced by my father, and by James Dine, Claus Oldenburg, and Julia Child as well. In the worlds of these workers, our understandings of tools are challenged. Dine fabricates and contorts his own tools; Oldenburg makes tools out of assorted materials and at megascales; Child—who presents herself as perfectly organized in her pegboarded workshop—uses the most wonderfully made devices to bring her great creations to life.

In the sketching exercise, I drew upon memories of my father, of gallery exhibits done by Dine and Oldenburg, and of Child's WGBH television show to visualize the hypothetical workshop of Rockefeller 3rd. The tools became dominant, essential, organized, clean, as does the small building that is the workshop; clean lines, the pegboard grid enlarged to determine wall locations, the edges of benches, and the like.

At some basic level, it is probably the case that Rockefeller 3rd couldn't fix a tractor, start a lawnmower, repair the heel of a shoe, or build a two-stall garage. Nevertheless, imagining him doing so, through the lens of my recollections of the father of my youth, brought me closer to understanding better what it was that Rockefeller 3rd was capable of doing, and did.

Wes Janz

143

Appendix 4

Mark Moreno

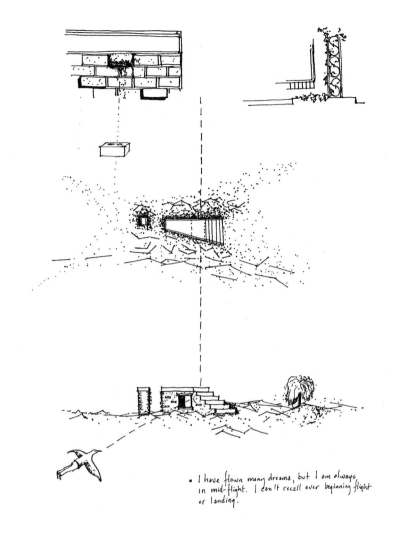

• I have flown many dreams, but I am always in mid-flight. I don't recall ever beginning flight or landing.

Character:　Myself
Act:　"Flying"
Place:　A Porch in My Childhood

Imagining and assembling the pieces for this drawing have entailed an oscillating process of sketching and remembering and analyzing. It began with remembering and will not have an end. A product, a place of contemplation, did emerge. In this case, however, I discovered something of personal import by juxtaposing all the pieces.

The discovery came by taking this sketch as a challenge to revisit a memory which I feared would produce unknown evils. In the process, it became evident and significant that I was always alone in my memories of the porch. This is ironic, because I have seven brothers and sisters, and the house was relatively small. I discovered that part of my identity lay in the meaning of the porch, for, as soon as I opened the door, I would cease to be an individual. The porch consequently always represents a place of security. It gives me the ability, the confidence, and the freedom to distinguish myself from my siblings.

It is here that I really begin to understand my own inclination to associate or identify with the elements of the design world. I have a tendency to personify the elements of design. To explore the relationships of the elements as if they have personalities is to have empathy for them, in that I can understand their immediate needs in a given context.

Memories, the makers of dreams, are powerful, sometimes elusive, and full of intrigue. They continually reconfigure that which makes personal identity. Consequently, memories and dreams are inextricably attached to what we, as designers, do. To what extent we are aware of this, of course, differs with the individual.

Dreams and memories often are confused when one is consciously remembering them. How often have we asked ourselves, "Was that a dream, or did I experience that at first hand?" To the best of my recollection, it is easier to mentally reassemble fragments of real-life experience than those of dreams. Likewise, a dream memory, with almost mythical power, transcends the dream itself. Consequently, one's conscious recollections and analyses differ according to what is being remembered.

I find that the major difference between remembering a dream and remembering an actual experience is that the dream memory retains a poetic mysticism. Sailing on a fifty-foot chartered yacht around the islands of Portland, Maine, is an experience I probably will not forget. With wonderful memories of company, food, and wine, with a Santana CD backdrop and an unexpected seal swimming by, I will say I need never sail a second time. This memory suffices for the rest of my life. However, having wings and flying in a dream over that water, engaging boat and the seal and water in ways unavailable in reality, I am enticed to analyze and search the soul for reasons.

In a book, the name of which I ironically have forgotten, the author *Mark Moreno* suggests a memory exercise that reaches into one's past to open doors to self-understanding. The exercise is a mental journey to one's childhood dwelling. With every step, one is to observe, with the mind's eye, every detail of the experience. Contemplating these realities floods the mind with mementos believed long since gone. I have attempted this exercise twice—once a year ago and once upon agreeing to participate in "Spatial Solitaire." Each attempt was a wonderful exploration—to a point. Each journey has taken me from the edge of the street in front of my suburban Texas home and to elements of extreme detail at the front porch. Both times, I was left wondering why I could not bring myself to open the front door of my house. My immediate conclusion was that I must be subconsciously suppressing some childhood horror. I had to dig deeper. I had to reach beyond those memory impulses. Sketching aided this process.

My nostalgic self can remember, in great detail, present and past conditions of the short walk to the house. Hovering over the lawn, he remembers the act of reaching out to grasp branches, to brush out of the path or to strip the leaves free. He touches the randomly corbelled bricks that provided climbing options for him as a child. He sees the bird's nest in the void in the uppermost brick course where a brick once lived. He hears the birds and climbs the ivy-covered trellis. He remembers what it was like to be little enough to sit on the low, narrow window sill and look back to the street.

This part of me remembers in one way and could go on for hours describing sensations. These memories would invariably lead to a nostalgic trip down "memory lane." However, the designer self (that is, the one with a background in design, who has a propensity for thinking and assimilating in a particular way and who has responsibilities and design intentions for the memories) already has begun prioritizing and analyzing associated words and phrases that have architectonic implications, i.e., Symbol, Public Mask, Threshold, Divider, Barrier, Gravity, Balance. This mental fork in the journey involves detaching from the memory and establishes a new agenda with a new kind of momentum.

Like the building of memories, design is a process of assembly that seemingly has no definitive end. Even at the completion of any construction, designers are forever rethinking and redesigning. Our intellect and schedules, or our business senses, compel us to filter and distill seeds of design, choosing those that will serve us to a beneficial end.

Appendix 4

146

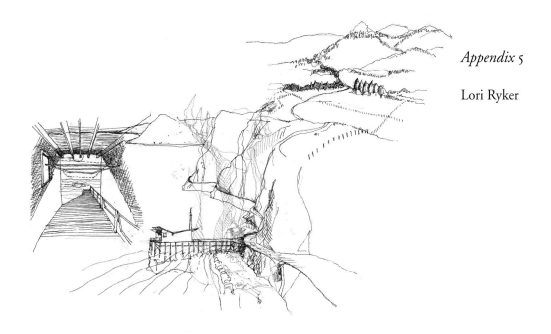

Character: Gretel Ehrlich
Act: Writer, Ranch Hand
Place: Place of Rest and Reflection

I began by selecting a character from my memory and indirectly my personal experiences: Gretel Ehrlich. Gretel has lived for some time in Wyoming, between the Big Horn Mountains and the Yellowstone region. She has made a life out of sheep herding and cattle ranching, while recording her experiences in words. Perhaps I chose her because I feel that Wyoming is my soul state, and she provides a link when I am so far away. I am at home in Wyoming and find rest there. Her words have reminded me how valuable it can be to leave the heaviness of life behind sometimes, to find yourself again. In thinking about Gretel, I think of Wyoming, and I think about the Big Horn Mountains, a place I know she and I have in common.

In the Big Horns, in heavy winter, I have been to visit a cabin that lies in Crazy Women Canyon. It would be a perfect place for Gretel. It would be a perfect place for rest and reflection. The canyon has Crazy Women Creek running through it. Where it winds its way out of the mountains, a cabin has been built on an edge of land, and a bridge which spans the creek carries a guest room and toilet. This cabin is quite comfortable in this place, nestled in the canyon of Crazy Women.

[How to tie this memory and Wyoming to Ehrlich's place?] Gretel was

147

struck by lightning a few years back in Wyoming, when she was out riding her horse. In her search to have her health restored, Gretel moved back to California to live with her parents. As I understand it, she has almost recovered but finds Wyoming to be distant. The house of rest is on the coast of California, along the winding Highway 1, which reminds me of the winding road into Crazy Women Canyon. Her house is only a shelter for rest and reflection, located upon a bridge set toward the horizon. The place stretches out to the world, to the ocean, in the same way I felt the Crazy Women cabin was making its place along the creek. The shelter opens up to the outside, losing the distinction between the realm inside and the world outside. The ocean, like the prairie, waves to her and me as we wonder when we will return to Wyoming.

I fly a lot in my memories; I see better this way. I remember quality of light: sharp in the winter; smells: clean; warmth: in the winter sun; cold: in the snow. I hear voices: laughter; rushing water; snow crunching. I hear myself silent, breathing, watching, reflecting, wanting this place for my own. It is the degree to which I sense these things in Wyoming that I attempted to recover when I played [the game of Spatial Solitaire]. Not the building, or material or details, but the world engaged and bouncing upon my intentions in material.

Appendix 5

148

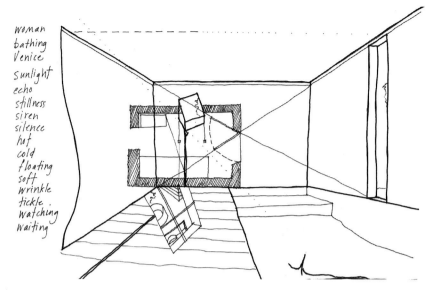

woman
bathing
Venice
sunlight
echo
stillness
siren
silence
hot
cold
floating
soft
wrinkle
tickle .
watching
waiting

Character: Woman
Act: Bathing
Place: A Bathroom in a Hotel in Venice

The act of drawing the plan of the bathroom begins to suggest a hierarchy of elements. There is the vessel or tub. A heat source—the radiator. A window allows air, light, and sound to enter from the street below. Another provider of water—the sink. There are the inhabitants, the bather and the observer.

The window. It is high and opens up completely. Other windows from other rooms are remembered and revisited. Looking down from above, being in the safety and seclusion of a raised room. Other tubs and water vessels are recalled.

From the layout of the original memory, the essential pieces suggest future alignments and extensions. The layout of the new space is determined in part by the devices of memory.

I believe we as designers look to our memory and respond to it in our work. We respond not only to our personal memory but also to a more universal one—that memory which is learned as part of our historical and theoretical training.

Memory is very powerful. It can stop us dead in our tracks. Just when we think we have forgotten, forgiven, intellectualized, and studied, we are reminded of our fragility, our past—the things we cannot change or escape from. It can be seductive, unpleasant, or frightening. It can render us speechless and frozen and unable to think. It can race across time and across space. We cannot escape this in our work.

Memory. To remember. To have come to the mind again.

Recognition. To identify as something that is known from before.

What is useful is to study the power in memory and recognition. Often designers will create something, only to discover later the object's similarity to something else. Was the designer copying? Did the designer only forget something from his memory? How is it significant that the new object triggers an old memory? Is it?

I believe it is. We are reminded of our past, of the passing of time. We recognize the more universal aspects of life. Of course, the question needs to be asked: what is the purpose of architecture? Is it the place of architecture to remind people of their past? I think that it is. Architecture is an art, and the purpose of art is to reflect and ask for a response to this life condition. By provoking a memory or a series of remembrances, architecture is provoking a response to itself. It is referring to a life lived. Memory and architecture are irrevocably linked.

Appendix 6

Character: Walt Whitman
Act: A Stroll
Place: Mountains and Valleys of the Northeast

Change of seasons.
The transformation of nature throughout the year.
The changes of color, light—visual.
The changes of temperature—sensual.

- Memories of stark, white, skeletal birches in winter.
- Memories of budding wildflowers, newborn birds, raging waters
  in spring.
- Memories of bright sunny skies, parched underbrush, ripe
  blueberries in summer.
- Memories of reds, yellows, browns, and greens in autumn.
  All are a part of the cycle of nature, the cycle of life.
  My life.
  Walt's life.

The river still runs; the trees still bud, bloom, and change; the mountains still rise for me as they did for a million other creatures. My character is

real but not living. He's been to the places I've remembered. We are all a part of the cycle of natural transformation: birth, life, death. The woods make this transformation yearly:

birth with spring,
life with summer,
descending to death with fall,
death with winter.

But their journey begins again and again. The birds return, the bears come out of hibernation, the flowers and trees bloom.

My memory is filled with important influences. Childhood is filled with winters in Wisconsin, where snow created a changing playground. Adolescence finds me on the beaches of the East Coast, with sand and surf to amuse me. Early adulthood (a place I intend to remain) finds me in the city, with its cacophony of sights, sounds, textures, and experiences. Here I learned about design. School taught me the history of buildings, the importance of practice, the communication of the built environment. Walt Whitman taught me the beauty of nature, the emotion of place, the celebration of life.

The path we travel is interrupted by these experiences. We pause at them when we search our memory, constantly revisiting their beauty. The river that runs continuously from the mountain through the valley is the datum. The profession of architecture is the river of the architect's life.

Through nature we sense peace, an understanding of the way things are. Our emotions are affected by the time of the year and the moment in the day.

The objective is to create space that accepts the natural order of change.

Appendix 7

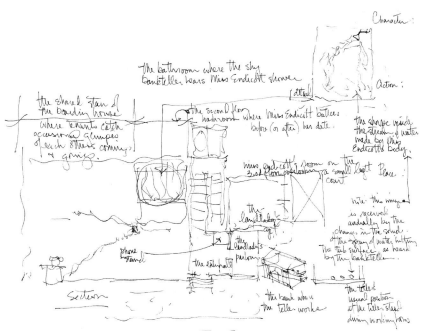

Appendix 8

Jim Asbel

Character: Miss Endicott, a long-lost friend, has gone off to London, where, residing in a boardinghouse, she remains out of touch with her anxious friends back home.

Action: Miss Endicott is called to the phone in the entry hall by a fellow boarder (a balding bank teller). She hears and considers the question of the caller's identity. She prepares to descend the staircase.

The staircase is only imagined by an anxious friend back home. It is an imaginative reconstruction from several period movies about U.S. servicemen dating young British girls during World War II. Upon this synthetic space are superimposed auditory and tactile sensations derived from staircases actually experienced by this friend. It is not the friend, by the way, who is calling on the phone. The friend, who in fact is imagining the entire scene, speculates that the caller is perhaps a new lover with whom Miss Endicott has become totally obsessed.

Appendix 9

Vince Canizaro

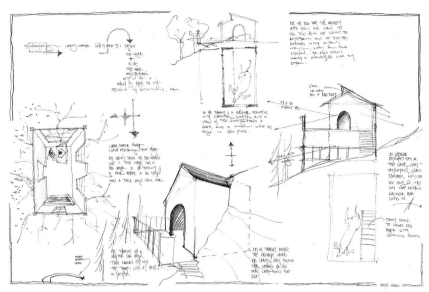

Client: Curious George's Dog
Place: A Dog House

In beginning the game of Spatial Solitaire, I could not get memories of past places out of my head, once I began to consider an act for my character Curious George. Curious George was hired by his dog to design him a new dog house. The story itself emerged from my past, as, prior to even thinking of becoming an architect, I made a house for my own dog.

In considering a place to begin, I thought back to my favorite design-studio space, which was a second-story single room, much like what I depicted in the drawing. This memory spurred me forward to consider schemes for the dog house as emerging from desirable places in my past: my house in Seattle which faced a ravine, my house in New York which provided the notion of clerestory windows and glass walls, and other micro place memories, which come in tidbits during designing and thinking.

This sensation is the same as that which I have while reading. When descriptions are of people and places, my mind naturally maps people and places I know onto the situation in the story, in the process altering them to fit the specifics, making new people and places. Virtual people and places, if you will.

154

Appendix 10

Ed Burian

The Ambiguous Reality of the American Southwest and the Construction of Memory: The Oro Valley Residence, Tucson, Arizona

INTRODUCTION

This residence intentionally engages the ambiguity which constitutes our daily experience of place in a postindustrial age in the American Southwest. Our experience of the Southwest and its meaning is formed both by the direct experience of the desert landscape, with its numerous sensuous qualities; and by representations of the Southwest and Mexico in films, literature, and television. True, the residence intentionally recollects memories of traditional vernacular building types in the Sonoran Desert, such as haciendas, ranches, and courtyard buildings . . . in terms of its organization on the site, traditional articulated transitions from public to private domains, and outdoor circulation under covered arcades . . . Even so, it utilizes compositional strategies from modern architecture, such as the interpenetration of exterior and interior space, and makes use of the possibilities of building with the materials and electronic technologies of our time.

The "construction" of our experience of the American Southwest is consciously utilized, heightened, and critiqued in the residence by a promenade through the building, courtyard, and desert site, which juxtaposes framed views into the "natural" landscape of the Sonoran Desert with "artificial" video screens, computer screens, electrical meters, automobiles. A heroic view of the desert landscape intentionally is called into question by those aspects of postindustrial culture which both make living in the Sonoran Desert possible and desirable, and alter our understanding of the "construction" of culture in the Southwest. Of course, what we call "natural landscape" also is called into question, as it is now anything but natural; it has been legislated, measured, and connected to the city via cyber and physical infrastructure.

BODY, MEMORY, AND TECTONIC EXPRESSION

While Baudriard claims the primacy of the reproduction over the real, I still would claim that the entire body, and not merely the eyes and brain, is the primary organ for experiencing architecture. Thus, the things recollected from memory include not only visual images but also the sensual experience of materials and their assembly—touch and texture, as well as sound.

Traditional masonry buildings are reinterpreted using earth-colored concrete block and mortar—an industrialized masonry assembly which responds to the technology of the present. The scale of the blocks records the effort of the individual craftsperson in their assembly. The metal roof which floats above the building simultaneously differentiates the walls as belonging to the earth and the roof as belonging to the sky, reduces the heat gain on the building, and helps move air between the two roofs. Saltillo floors and Arizona sandstone act as thermal maps and recall the building traditions of northern Mexico and the Southwest. The residence mimics the color of the landscape of the site and mountains beyond the exterior, while the interior is brightly colored and recalls urban vernacular architecture in Mexico.

Appendix 10

The recollection of traditional architecture in the Sonoran Desert is not merely visual, but is also body- and activity-oriented. Activities are programmed into the residence in terms of being able to circulate outside, dine indoors, and utilize a choreographed promenade through the building. However, these activities are reinterpreted in terms of contemporary culture. Covered places to sit outside and observe the landscape also include computer and video connections, while an outdoor bar to make margaritas and lemonade is situated adjacent to a lime and lemon grove.

Directions are acknowledged in the residence and respond to both ancient and contemporary rituals. Bathing, cleansing, and a breakfast area are oriented to the east; a dining terrace for watching sunsets faces west; and the lights of daily commuters in their automobiles and city lights may be observed to the south in the evening.

The house engages the reality of two working adults, in terms of the design of the kitchen, where two people can work at the same time, and separate study areas for each of the adults. The miracles of modern life are celebrated. A network of plugs for laptop computers, located throughout the residence (both indoors and outdoors), provide choices of where to "plug and play . . . or work." Each of the outlets and monitors is articulated to express the importance in contemporary culture of access to electronic information technology. The physical relationship of bodies to machines also is carefully considered, in terms of places to stand, sit, or lean; and in terms of furniture and built-in architecture. The articulation of these special places recalls the articulation of ritualistic activities in traditional architecture.

CONCLUSIONS: REGIONALISM RECONSIDERED

The relationship of dwelling to landscape in the American Southwest is increasingly complex in a postindustrial culture. On the one hand, it is difficult to deny the power of the physical and sensuous qualities of the Sonoran Desert, as experienced by the human body . . . and an awareness of its ascetic, poetic, and sublime qualities. However, this "heroic" understanding of the landscape is "contaminated" by the reality of postindustrial culture in the American Southwest and by the simulation of the Southwest and its landscape through television, cinema, and literature. Thus, this residence is an attempt to examine both these dimensions critically, to make an architecture appropriate to the complexity of our time.

Ed Burian

157

Client: Self
  Act: Projecting Houston
Place: Piranesi Drawings

The act of spatial construction, of drawing, is always a drawing from memory. But drawing is also a projection, an image extricated from the intermingling of multiple memories.

Since I first saw Giovanni Battista Piranesi's Carceri d'Invenzione in 1980, I have remembered and drawn and tried to understand the chiaroscuro depths of those incomprehensible spaces, mapping and recording the associative power of those precursors of modernism. Over and over, I sink into the map and the memory—obsessively, through and across and within time—to this momentary present in which I write and try to remember a conflation of memories into one drawing. Thus have I followed Piranesi's vision through an astonishing collapse of historical time and space and multiple personalities, with the perception of physical substance and the interpretation of interwoven text. In those shadowed interiors and infinite transgressions of space, filled with implements of torture, or instruments of scale and measure, or the mechanisms of construction, I found a dense, palpable ambiguity which denied closure, which questioned the singularity of form.

Eisenstein, Yourcenar, Robbe-Grillet, and Tafuri traversed this territory, exploring the intertwining immediacy of form and content, making indistinguishable the boundaries between drawing, thinking, and meaning in the simultaneity of Piranesi's spaces.

158

I found Piranesi in Eisenstein's films and in Eisenstein's obsession with Piranesi in "The Fluidity of Form."

I found Piranesi in Marguerite Yourcenar, as I traced her fascination with Hadrian through *The Memoirs of Hadrian* to "The Dark Brain of Piranesi."

I found Piranesi in Robbe-Grillet's ideas of the "new novel," through the collapse of representation and linear time in *The Labyrinth and Topology of a Phantom City.*

I found Piranesi in Tafuri's cryptic writings on revision and history in *The Sphere and the Labyrinth.*

I found Piranesi in Rome, among the reality of twisting ruins and the memory of Campo Marzio.

I found Piranesi behind every crumbled wall, in each half-completed space, and on random peregrinations through the ruins of Villa Adriana.

And I found Piranesi among the canals and streets of his Venetian birth-place, in winding forays through the collapsing splay of walls and façades, the reciprocity between the sudden turn to light and the walks into darkness. Mechanisms on display, the tension between activity and silence as one moves through time and through the city. In Tintoretto and Titian, in the medieval spaces which let only two buildings stand independent of the web of space made for the masque of life.

I drew, and still draw, to find the interstitial relationship between an active drawing through memory and conventional modes of the architectural expression of space through orthographic projection.

And this drawing is of a room in Houston, which is not a room but the underbelly of the suburb: the relentless concrete of the freeway. This is a drawing of walls which are not walls, or of continuously reconfigured containers which will become wall-like, where memories of all of these figures, events, experiences have become a search through light and shadow for Piranesi's ghost. All coalesce into a single drawing with the figures of instrumentality and modernity—the figures of the archaeologist, or the surveyor, or the architect. Here, or there, are the recording devices in a temporary house of memory, remembering, room by room, the interweaving of marks on paper and marks upon an architect's memory.

Scott W. Wall

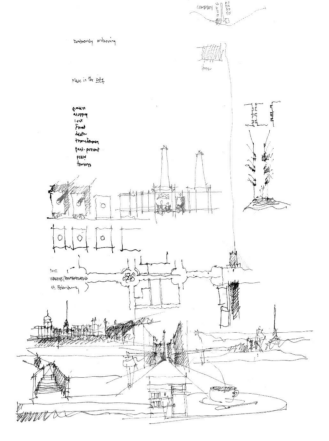

Place: Saint Petersburg
Character   Dostoevski

The memory of places has played a significant role in the way I approach design. Such memory can be applied literally, as in the design of a residential college in the Appalachian Mountains, where we intentionally attempted to recall the way the Italian hill town responds to its setting; but most often the remembrances are not so easily translated.

What I think is most important about remembering Saint Petersburg, through my own experience and through the writings of Dostoevski, is that the memories are rooted in a series of events and places rather than in a specific building or place. The connection of experiences, places, and events overwhelms the particular.

The notion of how one experiences places is something I have tried to bring to all projects that I am involved with, whether it be an urban project or a small-scale building.

160

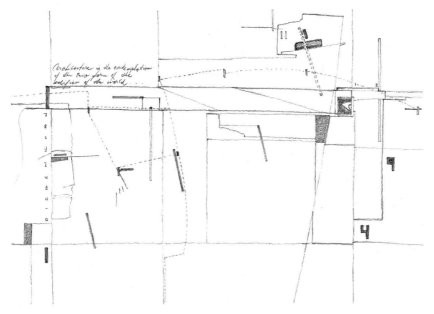

Fact and Implication; or, A 397-Word Reflection on an Unpremeditated Drawing

> I do not know how I entered
> I do not know well how to recount how I entered there . . .
> > —Dante, *Commedia* (*Inferno* I, 10)

> [Architecture as] the conception of the world as law-bound in the relation of simple elementary components, yet open, unbounded, and contingent as a whole.
> > —Meyer Shapiro, "On Some Problems of the Semiotics of Visual Art: Field and Vehicle in Image-Signs"

1. Drawing as Contemplation
   Memory and projection, representation and abstraction, *in*visible and *in*visible, form and *trans*form . . .

2. Move|Meaning (Form|Content)
   Dialectical signifiers of a built project: *Dante*|*Telescope House*[Zlowe]

ABSTRACT FORM

Painters	Diebenkorn, Gris, Mondrian, Léger, Radice

$$y = ax^2 + b + 18 \text{ (Georges Vantongerloo, 1930)}$$

Numbers 1:4:9:16| "Creations of calculation . . . a superior mathematical order" (Le Corbusier, Terragni)

NARRATIVE CONTENT/IDEAS

Astronomy   Architecture as observatory: *sacred space,* marked out for the contemplation|observation of reality. Architecture as optical instrument, device of orientation, as physical and *meta*physical site (Vitruvius: Architecture as the divine intelligence which orders the universe; Galileo: 01.13.1610; Io, Callisto, Ganymede, Europa, *Siderius Nuncius,* eye and optics, the telescope, seeing, and modernism)

Literature   The book as building and the building as book (Dante [*Commedia,* ca. 1307], Alberti [*De Pictura,* 1435], Mondrian [*Natural Reality and Abstract Reality,* 1919], Akroyd [*First Light*], Kubrick and Clarke [*2001: A Space Odyssey* . . . 1:4:9, TMA Monolith], numbers, astronomy, painting, ontology, Terragni's *Danteum* . . .)

3. Theme of the *Contingent*-Rectangle
   Boundaries, broken boundaries, dissipated boundaries, subboundaries, clear and ambiguous boundaries; framing, subframing, counterframing, interframing . . .

4. Figure|Field
   chess game (and subgame) of intercontingent fields and figures, subfields and subfigures, discontinuous and ambiguous figures . . . dissipation/concentration, extension/contraction, empty/full, center/edge, cut/intercut/countercut . . .
   The Knights Move (Shklovsky); *Violin* (Picasso), *papier colleé,* 1912 (cut, separate, shift, rotate)

Appendix 13

5. Plan|Section|Elevation
   Horizontal/vertical field reciprocity

6. Site|Sight Marking
   Markings of the visual field, of the *contingent* site|sight

7.   A Plastic System
     Prefiguring a visual|intellectual system of inter-contingent,
     self-evident, site-specific *relationships* . . . devices/techniques,
     materials, ideas . . .

All art tends towards structuring the contradiction between
that which appears and that which signifies between form and
meaning.
                    —Robert Sutzky, "ReReading Transparency"

Jef 7rey Hildner

163

Appendix 14

Thomas Sofranko

Character:	Judas Iscariot
Act:	The Last Supper
Place:	Iscariotic Bistro

Iscariotic Bistro is a risk-taker's place of repast. The straight and narrow path leads to a precarious landing. There, profound detachment serves as a gentle reminder of the need for separation and introspection, while simultaneously engaging the paranoid neuroses of every patron. Iscariotic Bistro: the perfect place for a zealous zealot's ego to enjoy a last supper.

Design attempts to make apparent. Through memory, a designer finds substance to make visible an abstract world comprised of ideas, intentions, and emotions. Design, as a process, does not occur in a vacuum. Architecture develops through the extension, transformation, and recombination of previously recorded scenarios. The mind operates like a temperamental recording device, alternately storing or ignoring all with which it comes in contact. The process of design begins with ideas composed from fragments or stored memories. In the words of author Tim Robbins, artists "recreate the world from the world." The world plays out in front of us and is carried with us as memories; these are used to recreate the world and allow the situation to play out again and again.

Our future shapes our past. Sitting at a drawing board, intent on "creating," one consciously or subconsciously pulls from memory files bits and pieces of past actions and emotions. The emotional/neurological process of remembering or returning to memories is a transformation process influenced by the passage of time. To some degree, memory is selective, but memory also offers the possibility of superimposing its fragments so that the whole is often greater than the sum of the parts. In memories, tangible and abstract exist in a constant state of flux, as structure and emotion change hands, and as past, present, and future coincide.

Design is the death of memory. The design idea, formulated from memory fragments, is a temporary construct often lacking the fortitude or clarity necessary for the designer to use it as an intelligible communicative device. Occasionally, however, an idea emerges between fragments with such precision and clarity that the conscious mind can extract it from the subconscious and the designer can make the memory concrete. In the design process, as ideas become tangible, the memory loses its translucent, transitory, multi-dimensional complexity—in effect, the memory dies and is replaced by a physical marker (the constructed architecture). This marker, much like a tombstone, remains as the residue of what once was.

Thomas Sofranko

Appendix 15

Mark Lochrin

Character:　Bugs Bunny
Act:　Negotiation
Place:　A Series of Backyards

The place stemmed from a memory of a series of backyards, adjacent to or near the house where I grew up. Also included are fences and front gates. The "stiles" represent openings in the fences or fences frequently scaled. Memorable trees, or trees that served as tree houses, are also noted. There is a sort of black screen, but I don't know what this stands for.

The low canopy of a neighbor's small orchard is there, plus another neighbor's television set and a pictogram of their plush, deep lawn. Yet another neighbor's tennis court is there, with an out-of-scale umpire's seat.

The gates and the ground on which the stiles and the umpire's seat rest are gateways to other realms, many of which seem to be subterranean. Perhaps a reference to Bugs' frequent burrowing in and out of situations.

The representation is more of a two-dimensional key to the literal location of significant memories within an actual territory of childhood play, as well as the suggestion that these locations possibly are doors to other trains of memory.

At a trivial level, all waking life is underpinned by memory, most of which appears to be subliminally present.

The relationship between memory of personal experiences and design is illusive. Individual memories, even those not invoked by a deliberate or dream-like act of mental revisualizing, appear to well up as an influential, but subliminal, tone. It is a tone which, in terms of appropriateness or adequate materiality, is not always well integrated into a design. I say this because, in almost all designers' works, there are themes of space and form and light that reappear, practically independent of the specific building situation under consideration. Often the designer is only dimly aware of the repetition.

However, some of the more creative work I have seen among students seems to stem from a conscious attempt mentally to re-image a situation, in the depth of its physical attributes, such as feeling the brush of clothes on a clothesline. This is a relatively rare act of imagination, often in an unconstrained moment, i.e., when at the drawing board. Usually, in people with an otherwise developed spatial sense and adroitness at composition, the present and convention crowd in before the lyrical past is heard. Individual designers' capacities consciously to recall prosaic or exotic occasions vary widely.

Another aspect of the impact of personal memory on a design (outside the solo studio project) is that it appears rarely to be articulated by a chief designer when explaining the tone of a projected design to other team members.

I personally subscribe to the constructivist or phenomenological hermeneutical school of thought which maintains that all learning is dependent upon remembered mental identities of things, and that these mental identities have overlapping characteristics and imprecise boundaries. That is to say, the stuff of memories is not fundamentally dependent upon words. This *Mark Lochrin* displacement and substitution of mental images, along with the ability to recall in physical detail the locus of past actions, appear to underpin creativity in design.

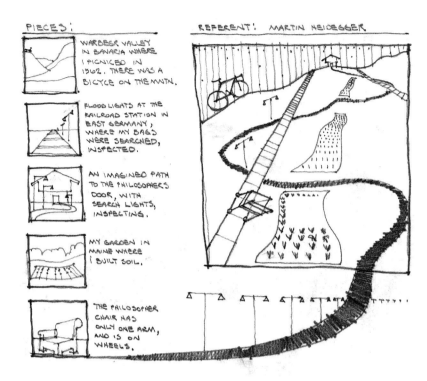

PIECES:

WARDESE VALLEY IN BAVARIA WHERE I PICNICED IN 1962. THERE WAS A BICYCE ON THE MNTN.

FLOOD LIGHTS AT THE RAILROAD STATION IN EAST GERMANY, WHERE MY BAGS WERE SEARCHED, INSPECTED.

AN IMAGINED PATH TO THE PHILOSOPHER'S DOOR, WITH SEARCH LIGHTS, INSPECTING.

MY GARDEN IN MAINE WHERE I BUILT SOIL.

THE PHILOSOPHER CHAIR HAS ONLY ONE ARM, AND IS ON WHEELS.

REFERENT: MARTIN HEIDEGGER

Appendix 16

Stephen Moore

Character: Martin Heidegger
Place: Philosopher's Home

I recognized when making my drawing of the Philosopher's Home that I routinely experience two distinct levels of memory in the process of design. The first level recalls a series of subjective, disconnected frames that emerge from personal history. The second level recalls more objective, abstract structures that emerge from cultural tradition. Separate from these two levels is a stockpile of formal antecedents, or exemplars—Palladio's Villa Rotunda, Kahn's Exeter Library, Le Corbusier's Villa Savoye, and countless other images—which designers carry around in their heads and which are the products of education. Although these exemplars are in a sense *remembered* in the process of design, they remain one-dimensional (meaning visual only) until experienced in some fuller sense. Having made many architectural pilgrimages in my life, I have experienced a few exemplars with enough intensity to produce lasting subjective memories. Five days of house-sitting at Wright's Fallingwater, for example, left a vivid memory of the hand-hewn stone floors at my feet, not in my visual stockpile of design "moves." Other exemplars that I have visited remain the collected views of a tourist. Leaving learned exemplars aside, it is the relation of the two perceived levels of memory that interests me here.

168

The first level of subjective memory—the frames that I recall in the process of design—is alternately filled by images, smells, sounds, or touches that seemingly are evoked by the conditions of a site itself. These resonances between the present and the past are phenomenological in nature—meaning that they cannot be explained in objective terms, only experienced and appreciated as a subjective form of knowledge. These memories are not quantifiable measures to which we have willful access, but are seemingly random connections to the categories of private experience that normally are concealed from consciousness. I have absolutely no idea why I connected Martin Heidegger to a bicycle that I have not recalled for thirty-three years. Such speculation is, without the skills of Jungian analysis, not a very productive enterprise. It seems enough to appreciate the possible mysteries that the relation might illuminate—both about Heidegger as a referent and about myself as a designer.

Sites also recall figures—the second level of memory that I experience in the process of design. By *figures,* I mean the *a priori* forms and networks implicit in the local conditions of the place itself. As soon as I lay an axis across representation of the site (say, from one hilltop to another), or draft the angles of the summer and winter sun, or place the project in an economic context, memory is triggered. This formal memory is not of personal history, nor of learned antecedents, but of Kantian categories—circles and squares, public and private, and so forth. The struggle for me as a designer—and, I suspect, for us all—is to *remember* the figures implicit in the site itself, to bring forth the *multiple* figures that are possible there, rather than to impose a single abstract order upon the site that is unrelated to what exists on the ground. In this sense, exploring a place through design is an act of cultural remembering. The structures of space and of society must be made present in our designing.

Both subjective memory and objective memory have two sites: the remembered and the rememberer. In the subjective, the site of the rememberer is key; in the objective, the site is cultural. Both memories tell us most about the rememberer.

There is, of course, a tension between these two kinds of memory—the subjective and the objective, the local and the universal. The romantic favors the former, and the modern favors the latter. Rather than accept either of these exclusive possibilities, I struggle to find an inclusive memory that operates within both categories of recollection, that dwells exclusively in neither the local nor the universal. To do so, we need access to both levels of memory—to the bicycle on the mountain and the twenty-five-square plan that orders my drawing.

Stephen Moore

Character: Mom
Act: Walking While Thinking
Place: Hanging Bridge Across River in Hometown of Santa Fe, Argentina

Human cognition and behavior are based upon our capacity to match new situations, problems, and solutions to those encountered earlier (i.e., recorded past experiences, knowledge). A particular mnemonic representation is applicable to a given situation because of certain features common to both that representation and the present experience. Analogies and inferences are the mental mechanisms used to make the necessary connection between the two. The result is that precise puzzle solving becomes, little by little, a way of seeing that opens up a way of doing. For, as Schön says, "Seeing this situation as that one, one may also do in this situation as in that one."[1] According to Schön, when a person makes sense of a situation he perceives to be unique, he sees it as something already present in his repertoire . . . [This means] to see the unfamiliar, unique situation as both similar to and different from the familiar one . . . The familiar situation functions as a precedent, or a metaphor, or . . . an exemplar for the unfamiliar one."

It follows that the essential nature of memory initially is perceptive, because it is only by seeing something else that memory becomes operational and thus useful. Yet, as soon as this has occurred, the perceptive function transforms a procedural or behavioral function (way of doing).

Memory consists of representations that are largely nonverbal and used as exemplars. The following definition of three types of thinking depends on their use of memory:

1. Remembering:
    Recalling of past events, experiences, information, etc.
    Remembering is knowledge-bound.
2. Reasoning:
    Systematic (often linear) association.
    Unfolding of ideas, information, images, etc., following a preexisting logical order.
    Reasoning is largely knowledge-bound (reasoning is remembering following a logic process).
3. Imagination:
    Arational (nonlinear) association.
    Unfolding of ideas, information, images, etc., following a loose order.
    Imagination is not knowledge-bound (imagination is remembering following a nonlogical process).

Within invention-driven studio pedagogy (popular since modernity), the initial stages of design are driven by imagination (design idea generation), while the later stages are driven by reasoning. Within a precedent/typology-driven pedagogy, reasoning prevails during the beginning stages of design (imagination is circumscribed to the development of a type, thus turning into a reasoning), but remembering and reasoning prevail during the later stages.

Memory is knowledge. Memory can be used to help simulate new situations by means of exemplars. Memory liberates and traps: it liberates by giving a framework for action, from which such action then may depart; it traps, as the framework may be so strong that it proves impossible to break free of it. Memory *is*, to an extent, the universe of discourse. It establishes the reference point from which criteria and exemplars are utilized to accept/reject/develop ideas. Memory structures and shapes our perception of reality. Memory is generated and generates (supports and is supported by) a set of social habits used in everyday life to ensure social interaction (predictability). A good design use of memory should avoid its direct, literal utilization; otherwise, the mind avoids inquiry and falls into mechanical, uncritical behavior and stereotypes. The problematization of memory is essential. One

Julio Bermúdez

does it by de-framing the context of thought, so that memory has to be used in a different, indirect manner. Design, as a process of action/inquiry, develops a memory.

The socially approved way of utilizing memory in design is through the use of precedents implying the continuity/critique of a language and typology. Memory is a constructive process/product. It is interfacial: both subjective and objective.

Appendix 17

172

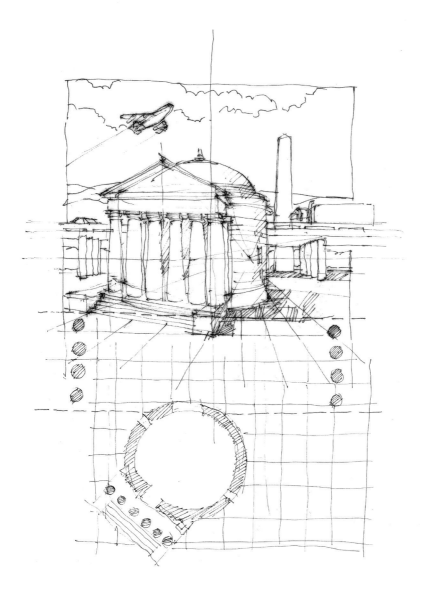

STUFF SHOWS UP

The question of memory's utility for the designer is an intriguing one, though it might well be understood as something which too often is taken for granted—a kind of instinctive, unconscious reflex which generally just "shows up" without deliberate or critical forethought. Which may be all for the best. The designer's use of memory is a bit like hosting an elegant cocktail party. You send out a slew of invitations, noting time, location, and some inkling of the purpose of the event, and then sit back and wait, not entirely sure of the response you will receive. To be sure, you can expect some old cronies to show up. Some trusted and familiar friends are welcome. Others, who arrive mostly out of a compelling sense of social obligation, are perhaps not so welcome. Either (or both, for that matter) offer an expected presence, be it reassuring or troubling, which nevertheless may also be tiresome, for you have seen all these people many times before and have grown ever so weary of their canned cocktail rap. You truly long for something new to stir things up this time around.

Hopefully, somebody else (somebody unexpected) shows up: perhaps the companion of an invited guest; or a chance acquaintance you invited for a lark; or, best of all, a party crasher. The unexpected guest offers the opportunity for something new to occur: an interesting twist on a long-standing debate, a new and refreshing point of view or opinion, perhaps even a spirited though minor altercation among the players present.

At least that's what you hope for: the convergence, on one particular evening, of the familiar and the unexpected, both coalescing to produce something unique or intriguing or, on a rare occasion, something absolutely spectacular.

Sometimes it happens. And sometimes it doesn't.

And that, I would guess, is how memory works for the designer. Stuff shows up. Some of it is expected. Some of it isn't. Sometimes the two mate in curious or interesting ways which yield something of value. And sometimes they don't.

I would further guess (now completely overextending the metaphor) that really good designers tend to have more really good parties, because they have opened their minds up to the possibilities of memory's uninvited suggestion. And not-so-good designers keep having not-so-good parties, because they are not yet willing to trust the useful idiosyncrasies of memory's happenstantial nature. They don't yet appreciate that stuff just shows up.

Incidentally, on the sketch I made for you, it seems pretty clear to me that, on the occasion of your request, nothing showed up.

Appendix 18

174

1. Susanne Langer, *Philosophy in a New Key* (Cambridge, Mass.: Harvard University Press, 1957); Susanne Langer, *Feeling and Form* (New York: Charles Scribner's Sons, 1953); Gerald Edelman, *Bright Air, Brilliant Fire: On the Matter of Mind* (New York: Basic Books, 1992).

2. William Brewer, "What Is Recollective Memory?" in *Remembering Our Past: Studies in Autobiographical Memory,* ed. D. C. Rubin, (Cambridge, England: Cambridge University Press, 1996), 19–66.

3. B. Smith, *Memory* (London: Allen and Unwin, 1966).

4. Brewer, "What Is Recollective Memory?"

5. Martin A. Conway, "Autobiographical Knowledge and Autobiographical Memories," in *Remembering Our Past: Studies in Autobiographical Memory,* ed. D. C. Rubin (Cambridge, England: Cambridge University Press, 1996), 67–93.

6. Ibid., 88.

7. Brewer, "What Is Recollective Memory?" 37.

8. Frances Downing, "Image Banks: Dialogues Between the Past and the Future," *Environmental and Behavior* 4 (1992): 441–70.

9. Langer, *Philosophy.*

10. Ibid.

11. Edelman, *Bright Air,* 125.

12. Ibid., 130.

13. Ibid., 75.

14. Aldo Rossi, *A Scientific Autobiography* (Cambridge, Mass.: MIT Press, 1981), 62.

15. Edelman, *Bright Air,* 203.

16. Marcel Proust, *Swann's Way,* trans. C. K. Scott Moncrieff (1928; reprint, New York: Random House, 1970).

17. Ibid., 35.

18. Langer, *Philosophy.*

19. Proust, *Swann's Way,* 35.

20. Ibid., 36.

21. Conway, "Autobiographical Knowledge," 81–82.

22. Akmar Ahsen, "ISM: The Triple Code Model for Imagery and Psychophysiology," *Journal of Mental Imagery* 8 (1984): 15–42.

23. Proust, *Swann's Way,* 36.

24. Ahsen, "ISM: Triple Code Model."

25. Langer, *Philosophy.*

26. Proust, *Swann's Way,* 36.

27. Edelman, *Bright Air,* 171.

28. Ibid., 164.

29. Joe Self and I ran 20-minute workshops at the American Collegiate Schools of Architecture Southwest Regional Conference, Austin, Texas, Oct. 29–30, 1995, and at the 11th National Conference on the Beginning Design Student, American Collegiate Schools of Architecture, Fayetteville, Arkansas, Apr. 8–10, 1994.

30. Langer, *Feeling and Form,* 96.

Notes

31. George Lakoff and Mark Johnson, *Metaphors We Live By* (Chicago: University of Chicago Press, 1980).

32. Mildred F. Schmertz, "A New 'House' for the American Academy of Arts and Sciences Designed by Kallman, McKinnell and Wood," *Architectural Record* 11 (1981): 79–87.

33. Edelman, *Bright Air.*

CHAPTER 2. DOMAINS OF PLACE EXPERIENCE

1. Langer, *Feeling and Form;* Ahsen, "ISM: Triple Code Model," 15–42.

2. Robert Solomon, *Phenomenology and Existentialism* (Savage, Md.: Rowman and Littlefield, 1980).

3. Ibid., 32.

4. Edelman, *Bright Air,* 153.

5. Brewer, "What Is Recollective Memory?" 31.

6. David Rubin, introduction to *Remembering Our Past: Studies in Autobiographical Memory* (Cambridge, England: Cambridge University Press, 1996).

7. Conway, "Autobiographical Knowledge," 69.

8. Ibid., 88.

9. G. Kelly, *The Psychology of Personal Constructs* (New York: Norton, 1955).

10. Gaston Bachelard, *The Poetics of Space,* trans. Maria Jolas (1928; reprint, Boston: Beacon Press, 1964), 6. The reprint contains a new foreword by John Stilgoe.

11. Virginia Woolf, *A Room of One's Own* (New York: Harcourt Brace Jovanovich, 1957).

12. Susanne Langer, *An Introduction to Symbolic Logic* (New York: Dover Publications, 1967), 33.

13. Brewer, "What Is Recollective Memory?"

14. Ibid., 53.

15. David Littlejohn, *Architect: The Life and Work of Charles W. Moore* (New York: Holt, Rinehart and Winston, 1984).

16. Downing, "Image Banks," 441–70.

17. Conway, "Autobiographical Knowledge," 75.

18. Edelman, *Bright Air,* 104.

19. Langer, *Feeling and Form,* 263.

20. Edelman, *Bright Air,* 125.

21. Ibid., 130.

22. Eleanor Rosch, *Human Categorization,* vol. 1 of the series *Advances in Cross-Cultural Psychology,* ed. N. Warren (New York: Academic Press, 1977); Edelman, *Bright Air;* Lakoff and Johnson, *Metaphors We Live By.*

23. Earl Mac Cormac, *A Cognitive Theory of Metaphor* (Cambridge, Mass.: MIT Press, 1985).

CHAPTER 3. SIGNIFICANT FORM
OF MEMORABLE PLACE

1. Edelman, *Bright Air,* 166.

2. Robert Solomon, *Continental Philosophy Since 1750: The Rise and Fall of Self* (New York: Oxford University Press, 1988).

3. Solomon, *Phenomenology and Existentialism.*

4. Bachelard, *Poetics of Space,* 6.

5. F. C. Bartlett, *Remembering: A Study in Experimental and Social Psychology* (Cambridge, England: Cambridge University Press, 1932).

6. Mark Gelernter, *Sources of Architectural Form* (New York: Manchester University Press, 1995).

7. Ibid.

8. Langer, *Philosophy,* 15.

9. Ibid., 24.

10. Karl Popper, *The Logic of Scientific Discovery* (New York: Harper and Row, 1965).

11. Langer, *Philosophy,* 19.

12. Ibid., 21.

13. Langer, *Feeling and Form.*

14. Edelman, *Bright Air.*

15. Langer, *Philosophy.* A persuasive argument exists that understanding written language is hermeneutical in nature—that is, reading a piece requires a continual referencing between a part (the individual words) and the whole (the piece as it unfolds). While this most likely is true, text still unfolds in a linear manner. The whole is not understood holistically until it is completed; it is sequentially hermeneutical.

16. Langer, *Feeling and Form,* 145.

17. Ibid., 147.

18. Edelman, *Bright Air,* 108.

19. Langer, *Feeling and Form,* 41.

20. William Kleinsasser, *Synthesis 9: Essential Considerations for Architecture: A Comprehensive and Experiential Point of View* [coursebook] (Eugene: University of Oregon, 1995); Frances Downing, "Imagery and the Structure of Design Inquiry," *Journal of Mental Imagery* 11 (1987): 61–86; Frances Downing, "The Role of Place and Event Imagery in the Act of Design," *Journal of Architectural and Planning Research* 9 (1992): 64–80; Downing, "Image Banks," 441–70; Frances Downing, "Conversations in Imagery," *Design Studies* 13 (1992): 291–319; Frances Downing, "Memory and the Making of Places," in *Ordering Space: Types in Architecture and Design,* ed. L. Schneekloth and K. Frank (New York: Van Nostrand Reinhold, 1994), 233–50.

21. Brewer, "What Is Recollective Memory?" 41.

22. Conway, "Autobiographical Knowledge," 76.

23. Ibid., 78.

24. Solomon, *Phenomenology and Existentialism.*

25. Langer, *Philosophy,* 71.

CHAPTER 4. COMMUNICATING MEANING

1. Langer, *Introduction to Symbolic Logic,* 33.

2. Mac Cormac, *Cognitive Theory.*

3. Lakoff and Johnson, *Metaphors We Live By.*

4. Ibid., 70.

5. Edelman, *Bright Air,* 152.

6. Lakoff and Johnson, *Metaphors We Live By,* 71.

7. Ibid., 77.

8. Edelman, *Bright Air,* 150.

9. Lakoff and Johnson, *Metaphors We Live By.*

10. Edelman, *Bright Air,* 150.

11. Langer, *Philosophy.*

12. Edelman, *Bright Air.*

13. Lakoff and Johnson, *Metaphors We Live By.*

CHAPTER 5. INTENTIONAL FRAMEWORKS IN THE ACT OF DESIGN

1. Littlejohn, *Architect,* 49–50.

2. Hubert L. Dreyfus, ed., *Husserl: Intentionality and Cognitive Science* (Cambridge, Mass.: MIT Press, 1982).

3. William Reese, *Dictionary of Philosophy and Religion* (Atlantic Highlands, N.J.: Humanities Press, 1996).

4. Dreyfus, *Husserl,* 12.

5. Aron Gurwitsche, "Husserl's Theory of Intentionality and Consciousness," in *Husserl: Intentionality and Cognitive Science,* ed. Hubert L. Dreyfus (Cambridge, Mass.: MIT Press, 1982), 65.

6. Hubert L. Dreyfus, "Heidegger's Critique of the Husserl/Searle Account of Intentionality," *Social Research* 17 (1993): 28.

7. Ibid., 28.

8. Ibid.

9. Edelman, *Bright Air,* 68, 112.

10. Downing, "Conversations in Imagery."

11. Proust, *Swann's Way,* 16.

12. Rossi, *Scientific Autobiography,* 11.

13. City of Phoenix, Arizona, "Municipal Center Building Design Competition," Oct. 24–25, 1985, transcript, 38.

14. Rossi, *Scientific Autobiography,* 5.

15. Downing, "Conversations in Imagery."

16. Ibid.

CHAPTER 6. IMAGINATION AND INNOVATION

1. T. S. Kuhn, *The Structure of Scientific Revolutions.* Chicago: University of Chicago Press, 1970.

2. F. Caplan and T. Caplan, *The Power of Play* (New York: Doubleday, 1973); P. J. Qualls and P. W. Sheehan, "Imaginative, Make-Believe Experiences and Their Role in the Development of the Child," in *Mental Imagery and Learning,* ed. M. L. Fleming and D. W. Hutton (Englewood Cliffs, N.J.: Educational Technology Publications, 1983), 45–62; R. S. Fink, "The Role of Imaginative Play in Cognitive Development," *Psychological Reports* 39 (1976): 895–906.

3. Langer, *Philosophy.*

4. Lakoff and Johnson, *Metaphors We Live By,* 5.

5. Max Black, *Models and Metaphors: Studies in Language and Philosophy* (Ithaca, N.Y.: Cornell University Press, 1962), 236.

6. *Oxford English Dictionary: The Compact Edition* (New York: Oxford University Press, 1971).

7. Henry Glassie, *Folk Housing in Middle Virginia* (Knoxville: University of Tennessee Press, 1975); A. Gulgonen and F. Laisney, "Contextual Approaches to Typology of the Ecole des Beaux-Arts," *Journal of Architectural Education* 35 (1983): 26–28; T. Williams and T. Scofido, "Typology and Primary Elements," *Journal of Architectural Education* 35 (1983): 29–32.

8. Edelman, *Bright Air,* 160.

9. Mac Cormac, *Cognitive Theory.*

10. *Oxford English Dictionary.*

11. Langer, *Introduction to Symbolic Logic.*

12. Schmertz, "A New 'House,'" 80–87.

13. Rossi, *Scientific Autobiography.*

14. Mac Cormac, *Cognitive Theory.*

15. Rossi, *Scientific Autobiography.*

16. City of Phoenix, Arizona, "Municipal Center Building Design Competition," 1985, transcript.

CHAPTER 7. CONNECTIONS

1. Langer, *Philosophy,* 37.

2. Bachelard, *Poetics of Space,* 33.

3. Ahsen, "ISM: Triple Code Model," 15–42.

4. Edelman, *Bright Air,* 161–62.

5. Ibid., 167–68.

6. Langer, *Philosophy,* 240.

7. Bachelard, *Poetics of Space,* 99.

8. William Kleinsasser, *Synthesis 7: A Primer for Architects* [course manuscript] (Eugene: University of Oregon, 1984).

9. Langer, *Philosophy,* 251.

10. Rossi, *Scientific Autobiography.*

11. Langer, *Feeling and Form,* 40.

APPENDIX 17

1. Donald A. Schön. *The Reflective Practioner: How Professionals Think in Action.* N.Y., N.Y.: Basic Books, Inc., Publishers, 1983.

Note: Pages with illustrations are indicated by italics.

Index

Index

mental image processing, 69; and ordering of experience, 81–82; and precedents in design, 117–28, 170, 171–72; and reference to outside world, 64, 159; relationship to design, 83, 113–15; and sensate experience, 37; types of, 75–81; understanding through, 83, 143

Metaphors We Live By (Lakoff and Johnson), 75

mind-body relationship, historical approaches, 59–64

modal shifts in mental referencing, 76

modernity, focus on empiricism, 65

moments of being and places of self, 35

Moore, Charles, 84–85

Moore, Stephen: emotional impact of memorable place, 41; fluidity of meaning, 87–88; formal memory and Kantian forms, 111; subjective vs. objective memory, 91, 105, 107, 168–69

moral values and place experience, 22–23, 30–32, 79, 82–83

Moreno, Mark, 33–35, 95, 111–12, 129, 132, 144–46

multiple-meaning processing, 82

Myers, Barton, 98

naming of remembered places, 9–10

"natural intuition," 74. *See also* analogous thinking

nature and designer's relation to place, 38, *39*, 152

neo-Kantian construction, 64–67

Neo-Structuralist approach (Symbolism), 58–59, 65–71, 73–83

"nesting" and design, 96

neural Darwinism, 4, 58, 83

non-linguistic, memory as, 10, 70, 112, 167, 171

objective abstraction: as applied to place memory, 45–53, 105, 107, 156, 168–69; and intentionality, 91, 92, 93, 94, 100–102

objective reality: and categorization, 63–64; connections to subjective experi-ence, 133–34; Empiricism's claim to apprehend, 65; expressed object as part of, 15; and intention, 89; Kantian view, 59; pragmatic view of, 93; vs. subjective experience in design, 13, 62, 91, 104–12, 168–69

objects of experience: Husserl's view, 60; as intended, 88–89; mental imagery as virtual, 15, 67, 83

observation, empirical, and rise of mathematics, 65–66

Olímpico, Teatro, 125

ontology, phenomenological approach, 60–62

ordering of experience. *See* categorization

orientational metaphors, 75, 76–78

parables, memories as, 16, 22, 133

particular vs. transcendental self, 59–60

past and future. *See* time

patterns. *See* analogous thinking; meta-phorical thinking

perception, mental imagery's role in, 56, 62–63. *See also* sensate experience

personification metaphors of place, 78–79

phenomenology, historical review, 60–62

Philosophy in a New Key (Langer), 4, 58, 64–65, 67

physical aspects of memory, 4, 56–57, 58, 83, 133–34

Piaget, Jean, 63–64

place metaphors, 76–81

place types, 48–49, 104

Poetics of Space, The, (Bachelard), 61

Popper, Karl, 65

positivism, 63

pragmatic approach to design process, 4, 93, 105, 115, 131

precedents in design process, 114, 117–30, 170, 171–72

pre-rationative nature of symbol making, 66

presentational theory of imagination, 11, 68, 69, 71–72

primary consciousness, 12, 13, 56, 82–83

professional vs. student architectural designers, 45–46, 53–55, 74, 91, 101–102

Index

SARA AND JOHN LINDSEY
SERIES IN THE ARTS AND HUMANITIES

Barnstone, Howard. *The Galveston That Was.* 1999.

Culbertson, Margaret. *Texas Houses Built by the Book: The Use of Published Designs, 1850–1925.* 1999.

George, Mary Carolyn Hollers. *O'Neil Ford, Architect.* 1992.

Houghton, Dorothy Knox Howe; Barrie M. Scardino; Sadie Gwin Blackburn; and Katherine S. Howe. *Houston's Forgotten Heritage: Landscape, Houses, Interiors, 1824–1914.* 1998.

Kelsey, Mavis P., Sr. *Twentieth-Century Doctor: House Calls to Space Medicine.* 1999.